Editorial Project Manager
Lorin Klistoff, M.A.

Editor in Chief
Karen J. Goldfluss, M.S. Ed.

Cover Artist
Tony Carrillo

Illustrator
Kevin McCarthy

Art Coordinator
Renée Christine Yates

Art Manager
Kevin Barnes

Imaging
Leonard P. Swierski

Publisher

Mary D. Smith, M.S. Ed.

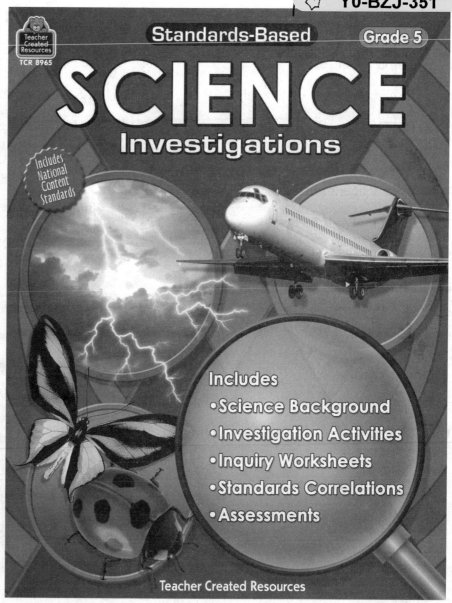

Standards-Based · **Grade 5**

TCR 8965

SCIENCE
Investigations

Includes National Content Standards

Includes
- •Science Background
- •Investigation Activities
- •Inquiry Worksheets
- •Standards Correlations
- •Assessments

Teacher Created Resources

Author
Robert W. Smith

Teacher Created Resources, Inc.
6421 Industry Way
Westminster, CA 92683
www.teachercreated.com

ISBN: 978-1-4206-8965-5

© 2009 Teacher Created Resources, Inc.
Made in U.S.A.

Teacher Created Resources

Table of Contents

Table of Contents

Introduction

The *Standards-Based Science Investigations* series is designed to introduce the vital concepts of modern science to elementary school students in imaginative, effective, and easily understood terms. The series is carefully arranged to spiral essential science ideas through the grades, building upon the students' prior experiences in the classroom and in life. This constructivist approach allows students an opportunity to do carefully modeled experiments and then to extend these hands-on activities with investigations of their own.

Every investigation is introduced with at least two pages of instructional text, which expresses the essential science concepts of the unit in clear, simple, and correct scientific and age-appropriate language. The explanations are carefully geared to the students' grade level and the level of intellectual development usual for that age.

These introductions are expressly designed to enhance students' skills for reading in the content area. Reading comprehension of basic textual materials, content vocabulary development, and fluency are addressed in each of the chapters. The "Did You Know That . . . ?" statements previewing each unit are designed to attract and maintain the interest of the reader. Specific content vocabulary is highlighted in every unit and explained in accurate and easy-to-understand terms. Major facts within each text are highlighted and reviewed at the end of each unit in the "Facts to Remember" section.

After the instructional text, there are student activity pages. The activities and concepts chosen at each grade level are generally aligned with the framework and suggestions of the National Science Education Standards and match most state guidelines. Each grade level book has activities and concepts from the life sciences, physical science, and earth science. Many readings have important historical and biographical notes as well. The correct approach to scientific investigation is routinely used at every grade level with each increase in grade level supporting greater complexity and sophistication in science understanding and hands-on experimentation.

The Student Inquiry Activities at the end of most units are designed to provide several structured approaches to inquiry investigations by individuals or teams of students. They offer brainstorming suggestions and questions to investigate, which lead to the development of inquiry questions by the students followed by suggestions for getting started. Students will then pursue their individual inquiry investigations using the Student Inquiry Worksheets (located at the beginning of the book) to facilitate and focus their investigations.

In summary, the *Standards-Based Science Investigations* series is designed to make science literally come alive in your classroom and take root in the minds of your students. Enjoy using this book with your students and look for other books in this series.

Locating Simple Science Materials

Almost all of the materials used for investigations in this book are easily available at school, from local stores, or brought from home by children. A few science tools, such as magnifying glasses and eyedroppers, are inexpensively obtained from science supply houses. This page lists the materials used in the book and suggested sources. Supplies, such as scissors, paper, math compasses, rubber bands, construction paper, index cards, and metric sticks, usually available at schools, are omitted.

Materials	Suggested Sources
magnifying glasses	science supply
thermometers	home/science supply
litmus paper	science supply
corks	home/science supply
light prisms	science supply
small mirrors	home/science supply
magnetic compass	home/science supply
flashlight bulbs	science supply
insulated wire	craft store/hardware
goldfish	pet store
guppies	pet store
fish food	pet store
crickets	pet store
ladybugs	home/plant nursery
chicken starter mash	pet store
field guides	libraries/book stores
almanacs	libraries/book stores

Locating Simple Science Materials

Below are common materials available from home, grocery stores, and local stores.

Materials	Suggested Sources
assorted insects	home
pond water	home/neighborhood
clothing iron	home
bones	home
water bottles	home
children's toys	home
x-rays	home/medical offices
bussing tray	large chain store
funnels	home/large chain store
wood skewers	large chain store/grocery
rough sandpaper	large chain store/painting supply
clear plastic cups	grocery/large chain store
fishing line	large chain store/sports shop
aquarium/fish bowl	pet store/home/large chain store
washers	builder's/large chain store
aquarium gravel	pet shore/large chain store
flashlights	large chain store/home
mesh screening	pet store/build's supply
plastic tubing	builder's/large chain store
ink pad	stationary/large chain store
modeling clay	large chain store
balloons	large chain store/grocery
straight pins	large chain store/grocery
masking tape	large chain store
batteries	home/large chain store
push pins	large chain store
salt	grocery
dish soap	grocery/large chain store
vegetable oil	grocery/large chain store
toothpicks	grocery/large chain store
clear packing tape	large chain store
cotton swabs	grocery/large chain store
food coloring	grocery
straws	grocery/large chain store
paper cups	grocery/large chain store
plastic silverware	grocery/large chain store
aluminum foil	grocery/large chain store
vinegar	grocery/large chain store
lemon juice	home/grocery
baking soda	grocery/large chain store
tea	home/large chain store

Standards Correlation

The 5th through 8th grade National Science Education Standards provide a powerful framework for employing the very best practices in science education. They provide broad and inclusive guidelines for the material to be taught in the physical sciences with special emphasis on matter and energy, the properties of motion and forces, and the transfer of energy. Education in the life sciences deals with the broad areas of the structure and function of living systems, the regulation and behavior of organisms within an environment, and the nature of heredity. Earth science education focuses on the structure of the earth, the history of the planet, and Earth's place in the solar system.

The most fundamental aspect of the NSE standards, however, is its primary focus on the inquiry method of science instruction. Students use their skills in reading and in doing hands-on experiments to inquire deeply into chosen avenues of science exploration. They move beyond simple explanations and experiments with pre-determined outcomes. The inquiry approach is by definition open-ended and subject to unexpected results. It requires a good deal of rigor in applying scientific processes.

These inquiries have many facets. They help students identify appropriate questions for scientific investigations. They require students to design and conduct a scientific investigation that is rigorous, detailed, multi-faceted, and thorough. Inquiry activities develop student intellectual tools in gathering and analyzing data. They help students make predictions and draw appropriate conclusions. Critical thinking and logical sequencing are a part of the student's learning curve as are opportunities to cooperate with other students.

Students also learn to apply new technologies to their scientific learning both in the use of available computer applications and multiple sources of information. Students learn to internalize the essential contributions of modern science to the preservation of life and the protection of the environment. The broad range of modern science study is designed to make an impact on each student's life and his or her attitudes toward all forms of life. Students must perceive science as a human endeavor with a long history and great potential for making a positive impact on the future.

Instruction in this text matches all of these disparate strands of science education by providing important content knowledge, interesting hands-on projects, and challenging inquiry activities designed to help students internalize their learning.

Standards Correlation

Science as Inquiry (Content Standard A)

As a result of activities in grades 5–8, all students should develop
- Abilities necessary to do scientific inquiry
- Understanding about scientific inquiry

(Units 1, 3, 4, 5, 9, 10, 11, 12, 13, 14, 15, 16, 17)

Physical Science (Content Standard B)

As result of their activities in grades 5–8, all students should develop an understanding of
- Properties and changes of properties in matter
- Motions and forces
- Transfer of energy

(Units 1, 6, 7, 8, 9, 10, 11, 12, 13, 14, 15, 16, 17)

Life Science (Content Standard C)

As a result of their activities in grades 5–8, all students should develop an understanding of
- Structure and function in living systems
- Reproduction and heredity
- Regulation and behavior
- Populations and ecosystems
- Diversity and adaptations of organisms

(Units 2, 3, 4, 5, 16, 17)

Earth and Space Science (Content Standard D)

As a result of their activities in grades 5–8, all students should develop an understanding of
- Structure of the earth system
- Earth's history
- Earth in the solar system

(Units 1, 6, 7, 8, 9, 12, 13, 14, 16, 17)

Science and Technology (Content Standard E)

As a result of activities in grades 5–8, all students should develop
- Abilities of technological design
- Understanding about science and technology

(Units 1, 2, 3, 4, 5, 6, 7, 8, 9, 10, 11, 12, 13, 14, 15, 16, 17)

Science in Personal and Social Perspectives (Content Standard F)

As a result of their activities in grades 5–8, all students should develop an understanding of
- Personal health
- Populations, resources, and environments
- Natural hazards
- Risks and benefits
- Science and technology in society

(Units 1, 2, 3, 4, 5, 6, 7, 8, 9, 10, 11, 12, 13, 14, 15, 16, 17)

History and Nature of Science (Content Standard G)

As a result of their activities in grades 5–8, all students should develop an understanding of
- Science as a human endeavor
- Nature of science
- History of science

(Units 1, 2, 3, 4, 5, 6, 7, 8, 9, 10, 11, 12, 13, 14, 15, 16, 17)

*All standards listed above are from *National Science Education Standards* (Copyright 2005 National Academy of Sciences, Content Standards: 5–8)

Thinking About Inquiry Investigations

 ## IMPORTANCE OF INQUIRY SCIENCE

Reading about science is important because students should be well versed in the content and language of science. Replicating and performing science experiments designed to illustrate scientific phenomenon is vital to enabling students to understand scientific principles and properties. This hands-on science component creates an interest in and understanding of the physical world in all its varied manifestations.

The apex of scientific learning, however, is the inquiry process of scientific investigation. Scientists use this procedure to investigate the ideas, events, and phenomena in science that they don't understand or haven't seen documented. In these investigations, scientists state the problem to be solved or the question to be answered. They design very specific investigations and experiments to test their own possible solutions to the problem or answers to the question.

 ## FAILURE ISN'T FAILURE

More often than not, scientists do not prove their stated hypothesis or even answer the question. However, most such investigations add to the information known about a subject in some way. It is important that students recognize that inquiry science and most original science experimentation fails. It takes many investigations to create a light bulb, to learn the living habits of an insect, to find a form of bacteria, or to map the migration range of a species of birds.

 ## SETTING THE PARAMETERS

Teachers need to set some limitations before introducing inquiry activities. These would involve sensible safety factors and limitations. Teachers should also set the specific expected behaviors required during an inquiry science period. These periods are often noisy and filled with conversation and discussion. Stress that discussions be pertinent to science and that all students must be involved and on task. Point out that investigations must involve reasonable topics and materials. Students will not have whales, elephants, electron microscopes, or jet liners in the classroom.

Thinking About Inquiry Investigations

 **TIMING**

Students need time to do inquiry investigations. Brainstorming, planning, and creative thinking are central to doing the investigations. In addition to building some of this focused thinking into the class schedule, expect some or much of the actual investigation to be done at home. Try to create a schedule specifying when each part of the investigation must be finished. You don't want it rushed at the end.

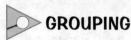 **GROUPING**

This type of science investigation can often work most effectively with teams of two students working together on brainstorming and planning. Their exchange of ideas and suggestions often speeds up the early stages of an inquiry. They are often able to complement, motivate, and support each other. Groups of more than two students often have some students uninvolved or frustrated. Some individual students work really well on their own, and this is a good time to let a child work alone if he or she is so inclined. You may be better at choosing effective, successful teams than students will be.

 TEACHER INPUT

You need to be an advisor making suggestions, offering encouragement, and focusing attention on the project. You are a facilitator helping your students solve problems of logistics, available materials, and personality disputes. It takes a kind of light hand to keep kids focused on the task without telling them what will happen. Ask students pertinent questions rather than telling them what will happen or what can't be done.

 MATERIALS

Children will have more trouble choosing materials and finding materials than any other part of the investigation. Help students choose reasonable and available materials. Give suggestions about possible substitute materials. You may need to help students realize they cannot do a specific project because there is simply no way to get certain materials or because safety is a concern. You will want to avoid dangerous chemicals, projects involving combustion, or dangerous tools.

Thinking About Inquiry Investigations

 ACCEPT THE MESS

Inquiry science is often a messy experience with lots of materials and rather rickety constructions and models. If the investigations are done in the class, try to allow enough time each day so each unit's activities do not go on for more than a week. If all experiments come from home on the same day, devote most of a day or two to the investigations and presentations. Things are less likely to get broken or damaged if they aren't kept waiting too long.

 ASSESSMENT

The rubric on the next page is a brief form with guidelines for the assessment of student work on inquiry investigations. It can be used as a checklist for judging the completeness of an investigation and the quality of the work. Students could also use it to evaluate their own work.

Be sure students know that they are not being scored on the success of the inquiry investigation but on the process. In these activities, "Did it work?" is not the criteria. The adherence to scientific process, originality of thinking, data collection, and a variety of approaches are the critical elements. The final grade is based on the number that conforms to the general level of the investigation.

 FINAL THOUGHTS

Enjoy the process. Encourage students to value their research and enjoy the inquiry experience. You and your students need to think of your inquiry investigations as an unknown path of adventure along the road to lifetime learning.

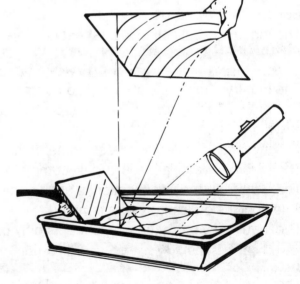

Inquiry Assessment Rubric

Final Grade: 4   3   2   1

Comments: _____

_____

4 Points — Advanced/Above Grade Level Expectations

The inquiry choice and investigation demonstrates original and creative thinking.
The brainstorming for the inquiry topic indicates a diverse range of potential topics of varying value.
The investigation demonstrates detailed planning.
The inquiry investigation is rigorously and completely done.
Some kind of data from the investigation is carefully recorded.
Carefully reasoned conclusions are drawn.
The inquiry investigation worksheet is carefully completed.

3 Points — Proficient/At Grade Level Expectations

The inquiry choice and investigation demonstrates some original and creative thinking.
The brainstorming for the inquiry topic indicates several potential topics of varying value.
The investigation demonstrates fairly detailed planning.
The inquiry investigation is completed.
Some kind of data from the investigation is recorded.
Some conclusions are drawn.
The inquiry investigation worksheet is generally complete.

2 Points — Basic/Below Grade Level Expectations

The inquiry choice and investigation demonstrates some thought.
The brainstorming for the inquiry topic indicates only two or three potential topics of varying value.
The investigation demonstrates some planning.
The inquiry investigation is largely complete.
The data from the investigation is unclear or limited.
One conclusion is made or attempted.
The inquiry investigation worksheet is only partially complete.

1 Point — Below Basic/Far Below Grade Level Expectations

The inquiry choice and investigation demonstrates little thought.
The brainstorming for the inquiry topic indicates few potential topics.
The investigation demonstrates little or no planning.
The inquiry investigation is largely incomplete.
The data from the investigation is unclear and not useful.
No conclusion is made or attempted.
The inquiry investigation worksheet has little or no information.

Part A: Student Inquiry Worksheet

▷ **Note to the Student**

Inquiry activities are an advanced level of scientific investigation. In these activities, you design the problem to be solved or the question to be answered and the methods you will use. Some inquiry activities are to be done individually, and others by teams of two or more students.

▷ **General Topic (Examples: temperature, snails, soil, etc.)**

_____

▷ **Brainstorming, Ideas to Investigate, and Questions to Answer**

Write down your inquiry investigation ideas here.

1. _____

   _____

2. _____

   _____

3. _____

   _____

4. _____

   _____

5. _____

   _____

6. _____

   _____

▷ **Thinking with Pictures**

Make sketches, drawings, outlines, or designs to help you think of ideas to investigate or to go with the ideas listed above. Use the space below.

▷ **Assessing Your Ideas**

- Cross out any question or idea that is too vague or unclear to test.
- Cross out any question or idea that is too complicated to test.
- Prioritize your ideas or questions. Put them in order from best to worst.

Part B: Student Inquiry Worksheet

▶ **Choosing Your Inquiry Investigation**

Choose the question or idea you personally like best. Write it here.

_____

_____

▶ **Assessing the Investigation**

1. What materials do you need to do the investigation?

   _____

   _____

2. What help do you need to do the investigation?

   _____

   _____

3. Can you do the investigation on your own and answer the question?

   _____

   _____

▶ **Importance of the Investigation**

Why does this question or investigation matter? What will you learn from the investigation?

I will learn . . . _____

_____

_____

▶ **Stating the Problem to Be Solved**

State the problem to be solved in a question format.

Example: What materials will magnets attract?

_____

_____

▶ **Stating the Hypothesis**

State your hypothesis (scientific guess) while clearly indicating what you think will happen. Use a simple statement.

Example: I think that magnets can attract most materials.

_____

_____

Part C: Student Inquiry Worksheet

▷ Planning the Investigation

Planning is a very important part of your investigation. First, break your inquiry investigation down into steps or parts. Ask, "What gets done first? What part of the investigation comes next?" Then record the steps in your investigation below.

1. _____
   _____

2. _____
   _____

3. _____
   _____

4. _____
   _____

5. _____
   _____

6. _____
   _____

▷ Making a Mind Map

Scientists need to convert the pictures in their mind into a sketch, design, layout, or map of what they think an inquiry investigation is going to look like as it progresses from step to step. Make a mind map with sketches showing what you think will happen in each step of your inquiry investigation.

Step 1	Step 2	Step 3
Step 4	**Step 5**	**Step 6**

▷ Anticipating Problems

Scientists doing any investigation need to look ahead and anticipate problems they might encounter in doing the investigation.

Which step might be the most difficult to do? Why? _____

_____

What will you do to overcome the problem? _____

_____

Part D: Student Inquiry Worksheet

▶ Do the Inquiry Investigation

This is the hands-on experimental part of the investigation. This part of the inquiry investigation involves using materials to make a model, gathering data to create a graph, or performing an experiment to prove a hypothesis.

▶ What You Did

1. State exactly what you did in each step of the investigation.
2. Draw sketches of the models and materials in the box below.
3. Record all data you collected in the "Data Record" section on the next page.

Step 1: _____

_____

_____

Step 2: _____

_____

_____

Step 3: _____

_____

_____

Step 4: _____

_____

_____

Step 5: _____

_____

_____

Step 6: _____

_____

_____

Part E: Student Inquiry Worksheet

▷ Record Data

Record numerical and statistical information in the "Data Record" section below. This data might be temperatures, lengths, weights, personal preferences, amounts, or anything that can be measured. Dates and times might also be important.

▷ Data Record

Date/Time   **Data**

_____   _____

_____   _____

_____   _____

_____   _____

_____   _____

_____   _____

▷ Graphing Results

Some statistics are much more effectively presented on graph paper. Use graph paper to make a bar or line graph of the data you gathered.

▷ Drawing Conclusions

Did you prove your hypothesis? Explain.

_____

_____

What went wrong?

_____

_____

What would you do differently another time? Why?

_____

_____

What did you learn from this investigation?

_____

_____

Part F: Student Inquiry Worksheet

▶ **Science Journal**

Scientists do written reports about their investigations so that other scientists and interested people can know what they did, how they did it, and what they learned. Write a complete report in the journal entry about your inquiry investigation for your fellow scientists (students and teacher). Be sure to stress what you learned and how the investigation was done.

▶ **Journal Entry**

_____

_____

_____

_____

_____

_____

_____

_____

_____

_____

_____

_____

_____

_____

_____

_____

_____

_____

_____

▶ **Illustrations**

Include any illustrations, pictures, or models that you wish.

Sample Inquiry Project: Making Wind Wheels

Materials
- *paper*
- *pencil with eraser*
- *large straws*
- *water*
- *straight pins*
- *thin straws*
- *clear plastic bottles*
- *index cards, tag board, or manila folder*
- *tape*
- *scissors*
- *ruler*
- *markers*
- *tissue paper*
- *paper clips*
- *decorative items*

Directions
1. Cut out the square on this page.
2. Slit the paper along the dashed lines.
3. Bend Point A to the center of the paper and tape it.
4. Bend Points B, C, and D to the center and tape each of them in place.
5. Push a straight pin through the center of the figure and into a straw or the eraser end of a pencil.

Making the Pinwheel Work
1. Hold the pinwheel into the wind.
2. Run holding the pinwheel up into the air.
3. Blow on the pinwheel.

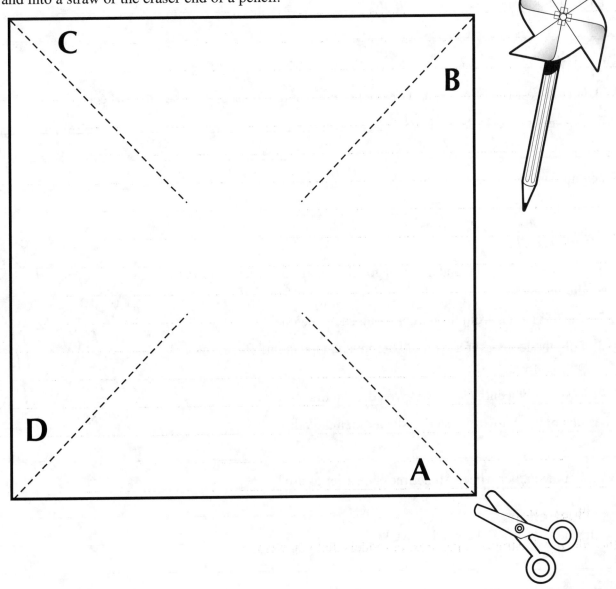

Sample Inquiry Project: Making Wind Wheels

Big Wheels

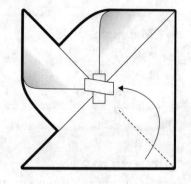

1. Use a ruler to draw an 8-inch square.

2. Draw the diagonal lines and cut 4 inches along each diagonal.

3. Fold the loops over as you did before and tape them.

4. Pin the wheel to a pencil eraser or straw.

5. Test this wheel the same way you did the first one.

Does the 8-inch pinwheel whirl faster or slower than the first one?

_____

Why is it a little harder to get started? _____

_____

What is the best method to get it moving? _____

_____

Try This

Make the largest wheel you can. Use the same method you used with the other wheels.

Why are larger wheels harder to use? _____

_____

When do the larger wheels work well? _____

_____

Mini-wheels

1. Cut a 3-inch square and draw diagonal lines from corner to corner as you did before.

2. Cut 1½ inches from the corner along each diagonal.

3. Fold the loops over as you did before and tape them. Pin the wheel to a pencil eraser or straw.

4. Test this wheel the same way you did the first one.

Does this pinwheel whirl faster or slower than the others?

_____

Why would smaller wheels sometimes be easier to use?

_____

Do they always catch the wind as well? _____

_____

Sample Inquiry Project: Making Wind Wheels

Wheels Away!

1. Make several of the designs illustrated on this page. Use paper for some designs. Try using index cards, tag board, paper plates, or manila folders for some designs.
2. Add paper clips, straws, tissue paper, and other decorative features. Use markers to add color.

Double Wheels

1. Use two of the pinwheels you already made to make a double wheel.
2. Slit both ends of a thin straw about one inch along each end.
3. Flatten the ends against the outside of one wheel and tape the wheel to the straw.
4. Cut a larger straw about two or three inches shorter than the thin straw and thread the wider straw over the thinner straw.
5. Tape the other end of the thin straw to another wheel. Make sure the loops or folds are facing the same way into the wind.

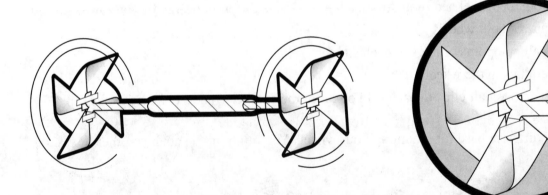

Using Double Wheels

Hold the double wheel by the larger center straw and face the pinwheels into the wind.

Why is it a little harder to get the double wheel to work?

_____

Will the double wheel work when you blow on it?

_____

Will it work when you run with it?

_____

How would you make a triple or quadruple wheel?

_____

Sample Inquiry Project: Making Wind Wheels

Working Wheels

1. Fill a large plastic bottle half full of water to make it stable.
2. Tighten the cap securely in case the bottle falls and place it outside on a table, if possible.
3. Attach your double pinwheel to the top of the bottle by taping the larger/wider straw to the bottle cap.
4. Make certain that the wheels can swing freely without touching the bottle.
5. Face the bottle into the wind and observe whether the wind will turn the wheels.

Improving Performance

If your wheel is not moving very fast in a brisk wind, check these points:

- Make sure that each wheel is taped vertically to the straw. You may need to add more tape or some reinforcement tape or paper clips to straighten the wheels.

- Lengthen the thin, inner straw if necessary. You can cut the thin straw, slit the ends, and thread the ends into another thin straw or half straw.

- You can slit the wider straw, if needed, to get it back over the inner straw. You might need a longer one of these straws as well.

Design Your Own Working Wheels

1. Make a second double wheel and mount it on a bottle. Use a different design of your own.
2. Add straws to one or both wheels.
3. You can add small pompoms or flags to each straw.
4. Add small paper clips to the wheels.
5. Try adding a chain of small clips to each fold or cut of the smaller wheels or wheels made of thicker materials.
6. Use an entirely different base for mounting your wheel. You might try a shoebox, other boxes, or giant soda cups.

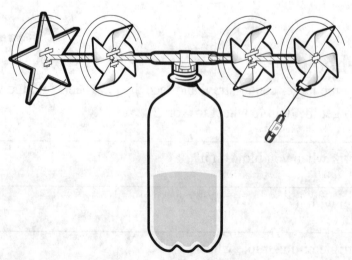

Classifying Living Things: Kingdoms

DID YOU KNOW THAT . . . ?

- *Some bacteria produce strong acids and actually eat stone. They cause damage to monuments and buildings.*
- *Lichens are **organisms** composed of green algae and a fungi living together as a single organism.*
- *At least three quarters of all known animal species are insects.*
- *Four out of every ten known animal species are beetles.*

SCIENTIFIC CLASSIFICATION

Scientists classify all living things within five categories called kingdoms: **monerans**, **protists**, **fungi**, plants, and animals.

MONERANS

This kingdom includes many of the simplest living things on Earth. These include more than 2,000 different **species** (kinds) of bacteria and more than 2,000 species of blue-green algae. These creatures are microscopic in size and made up of a **single cell**. They do not have a membrane to form a **nucleus** in the cell. Bacteria do not make their own food. Blue-green algae were the primary form of life for 2 billion years—from 3.5 billion years ago to 1.5 billion years ago. They produce most of the world's oxygen through the food-making process of photosynthesis.

PROTISTS

Protists are single-celled creatures which have a nucleus in the cell surrounded by a membrane. There are more than 57,000 species of protists. They include diatoms, amoebas, and euglena. You would see many of these with a good microscope. Ancient protists may have led to the evolution of multi-celled plants and animals.

FUNGI

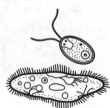

Fungi may have one or many cells. They do have a nucleus in the cell. They have a unique pattern of reproduction. Fungi do not produce their own food. They absorb food made by plants and animals. Some fungi are essential to the decomposition of dead plant and animal material and the recycling of those nutrients in nature. Other fungi obtain their nutrients (food) from living plants or animals. Fungi include mushrooms, yeasts, molds, rusts, and mildews. There are more than 46,000 species of fungi.

Unit 1

Classifying Living Things: Kingdoms

PLANTS

There are more than 248,000 different species of plants. Plants have many cells and are the basic food, directly or indirectly, of almost all other forms of living things. Most plants can make their own food through the process of photosynthesis using the green material called *chlorophyll*. This material in the leaves absorbs light from the Sun. Plants use this energy to combine with water and carbon dioxide to produce food and oxygen. Plants are divided into two classes: non-flowering and flowering. Non-flowering plants include seaweeds, mosses, ferns, and green, red, and brown algae. Flowering plants include grasses, trees, shrubs, cacti, vegetables, fruits, and flowers of many types. Most plants are unable to move, but they are carried by wind, water, and animals to many places.

ANIMALS

There are about 1,000,000 known animal species, although scientists think there may be millions more as yet unknown. Most animals are **mobile** (able to move about) for some or all of their life cycle. Animals do not produce their own food. They either live on plants or on other animals that eat plants. About nine tenths of all animal species are *invertebrates*—animals without backbones. These include worms, sponges, spiders, snails, crabs, jellyfish, and at least 750,000 species of insects. There are more than 44,000 *vertebrates*—animals with backbones. These include fish, birds, mammals, reptiles, and amphibians,

Facts to Remember
- *Living things are classified into five kingdoms: monerans, protists, fungi, plants, and animals.*
- *Monerans are among the simplest organisms and include some bacteria and blue-green algae.*
- *Protists are single-celled organisms which include diatoms, amoebas, and euglena.*
- *Fungi are composed of organisms that absorb food and substances produced by other living things.*
- *Plants make their own food through the process of photosynthesis.*
- *Animals are usually mobile and either eat plants or plant-eating animals.*

VOCABULARY

fungi—*organisms similar to plants which don't make their own food*

mobile—*able to move*

monerans—*single-celled bacteria and blue-green algae*

nucleus—*a small area in a cell which contains genetic material*

organism—*a living thing*

protists—*single-celled amoebas, diatoms, and euglena*

single cell—*an organism with only one cell*

species—*a kind of plant or animal*

What's What?

Directions: Label each of the living things on this page according to its kingdom: *moneran*, *protist*, *fungi*, *plant*, or *animal*. Use a dictionary to help you with unfamiliar words, and use the Internet to help you research the correct kingdom.

whale

_____

fern

_____

penguin

_____

green algae

_____

jellyfish

_____

moss

_____

mushroom

_____

frog

_____

rabbit

_____

pine tree

_____

bacteria

_____

spider

_____

amoeba

_____

blue-green algae

_____

mildew

_____

cockroach

_____

rose

_____

oak tree

_____

cactus

_____

butterfly

_____

ladybug

_____

lobster

_____

tiger

_____

salmon

_____

earthworm

_____

starfish

_____

diatom

_____

daisy

_____

euglena

_____

slime mold

_____

What Is It?

Materials
- *bones*
- *skin and hair fragments*
- *pond water with specimens*
- *leaves, bark, stems, flowers*
- *mushrooms and similar growths*
- *small garden creatures, such as bugs, worms, snails, etc.*

Directions

1. Gather as many specimens as you can find, living or dead. Collect bones, lawn mushrooms, bugs and small garden creatures, hair, webs, skin fragments, leaves, stems, roots, flowers, pond water or other stagnant water with specimens in it, and similar materials.
2. Draw a sketch of each specimen you have found and then describe each specimen.
3. Label each of the specimens you collected according to its kingdom: moneran, protist, fungi, plant, or animal.

Specimen #1 Sketch Description: _____ _____ _____ Kingdom: _____	**Specimen #2** Sketch Description: _____ _____ _____ Kingdom: _____
Specimen #3 Sketch Description: _____ _____ _____ Kingdom: _____	**Specimen #4** Sketch Description: _____ _____ _____ Kingdom: _____
Specimen #5 Sketch Description: _____ _____ _____ Kingdom: _____	**Specimen #6** Sketch Description: _____ _____ _____ Kingdom: _____

Classifying Living Things: Classes

DID YOU KNOW THAT . . . ?

● *Chickens can lay about 250 eggs a year.*
● *The largest fish is the whale shark which can grow to 50 feet long.*
● *It takes 22 months for the elephant baby to develop inside its mother before it is born.*
● *The fastest swimming mammal is the sea whale which can swim 28 miles per hour.*
● *The vampire bat eats only one thing: blood.*
● *Bats are the only mammals that can fly.*
● *The largest snake in the world is the anaconda which can grow 30 feet, longer than a school bus.*

CLASSIFYING PLANTS AND ANIMALS

Carolus Linnaeus, a Swedish botanist of the 1700s, created a system of **classification** for plants and animals based on similarities and differences for each **organism**. He described and classified nearly 8,000 plants and over 4,000 animals that were just about everything known to science at the time. Each living organism had two Latin names: genus and **species**. The genus referred to a group of similar animals and the species was the specific name of that kind of organism. His system is still in use today with modifications made by modern scientists.

CHARTING A FAMILY TREE

Kingdom All living things are divided into five kingdoms
Phylum Large groups of species with similar characteristics Examples: arthropods include insects, spiders, crabs, and animals with hard exoskeletons; mollusks include soft-bodied animals with shells; chordates include animals with backbones
Class Groups of animals or plants in a phylum with similar features Examples: mammals, reptiles, birds, mollusks, and amphibians
Order Groups of animals or plants in a class with specific features or behaviors Examples: carnivores (meat-eating mammals), rodents, marsupials, and bats
Family Groups of species with many similar characteristics Examples: felines (cats) and canines (dogs).
Genus Groups of very similar species. Examples: big cats
Species Animals that have the same physical and behavioral characteristics and can reproduce. Examples: blue whales, raccoons, grizzly bears, red squirrel, and coyotes

Unit 2 · Classifying Living Things: Classes

A NAME FOR EVERY ORGANISM

Every living organism is classified so that is has a specific name. The name is written in Latin. The first name is the genus and the second name is the species. *Panthera tigris* is the scientific name for a tiger. *Aplodonia ruf* is the name for the mountain beaver. *Rattus norvegicus* is the name for the common rat.

ONE FAMILY TREE

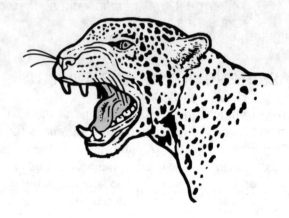

Kingdom—Animal

Phylum—Chordate

Class—Mammal

Order—Carnivore

Family—Cats

Genus—Big Cats

Species—Jaguar (Felis onca)

CLASSES OF ANIMALS

There are five major **classes** of **vertebrates** (animals with backbones). These include fish, amphibians, reptiles, birds, and mammals.

Reptiles

There are about 6,000 species of reptiles. Reptiles are covered with scales and are cold-blooded. They cannot control their body temperature. They are approximately the temperature of the surrounding air. Snakes, turtles, lizards, and crocodiles are reptiles. Except for snakes, most reptiles have four legs and a tail. Reptiles may live on land or water. Reptiles are especially well-adapted to living in dry, empty regions. A few reptiles give birth to their young alive but most lay eggs.

Classifying Living Things: Classes

CLASSES OF ANIMALS *(cont.)*

Birds

There are about 9,000 different species of birds throughout the world. Birds are warm-blooded animals. They are able to regulate their bodies at a constant temperature. All birds hatch from eggs. Birds have wings and nearly all species of birds can fly, although a few birds have lost the ability to fly and have adapted to different lifestyles. For example, penguins can swim using their wings, and ostriches can run very fast. All birds have feathers which help them fly by providing large surfaces for air to cover and keep them warm by trapping and holding heat. Birds have scales on their legs and toes. Most birds build nests to lay eggs in and raise their young.

Mammals

There are more than 4,000 species of mammals. They are the most highly developed class in the animal kingdom. Mammals have large brains and can learn from previous experiences. They are warm-blooded and thus able to control their body heat at a constant temperature. Most mammals are covered with hair or fur that traps and holds body heat. A few mammals, such as whales, moles, and humans have lost most of their hair. About 250 species of mammals called *marsupials* have short gestation periods and keep their newborn babies in pouches on the female body. Three species of egg-laying mammals exist. Most mammals have their young born alive. Mammals feed their young milk from the mother's body.

Amphibians

There are more than 4,000 species of amphibians. Most amphibians are comfortable on land or water. Virtually all amphibians spend some part of their live cycle in water. Nearly all amphibians lay their eggs in water. Most young amphibians go through a series of changes before adulthood. Young toads, frogs, and newts hatch from their eggs into tadpoles that live in water and have gills for breathing. They gradually develop legs and lungs and can live on land. Amphibians generally have sensitive skin that needs to be kept damp, or they will lose body water and die. Amphibians are carnivorous. They eat insects and other animals.

Unit 2 — Classifying Living Things: Classes

··

CLASSES OF ANIMALS (cont.)

··

Fish

There are more than 20,000 species of fish. They live in water—both salt water and fresh water. Some fish live in cold, ocean depths and others in warm tropical waters. Most fish have bones but a few, like sharks, have cartilage instead of bones. A few fish are live-bearers, but most fish lay eggs which are usually uncared for after the mother lays the eggs. Fish breathe oxygen in water by passing water over their gills. Fish are covered with scales and have fins for swimming.

Facts to Remember

- *All living things are classified according to their physical characteristics.*

- *Every living organism has two names: genus and species.*

- *Classification of an organism is organized by kingdom, phylum, class, order, family, genus, and species.*

- *There are five major classes of vertebrate animals: fish, amphibians, reptiles, birds, and mammals.*

- *Reptiles have scales and are cold-blooded.*

- *Birds have feathers and wings. They lay eggs and can usually fly.*

- *Amphibians usually live on both land and water at some time in their life cycle.*

- *Fish are covered with scales, live in water, and breathe through gills.*

- *Mammals are warm-blooded, usually have hair or fur, and have larger brains than most other animals.*

··

VOCABULARY

··

class—*groups of animals or plants with similar features*

classification—*organization of living organisms by features and behaviors*

organism—*a living thing, plant, or animal*

species—*a specific kind of plant or animal*

vertebrate—*an animal with a backbone*

What Class Am I?

Directions: Identify the class as *reptile*, *fish*, *amphibian*, *bird*, or *mammal* for each animal listed below.

blue whale

_____

emperor penguin

_____

African elephant

_____

manatee

_____

polar bear

_____

chameleon

_____

badger

_____

Pacific salmon

_____

king snake

_____

whooping crane

_____

desert tortoise

_____

golden eagle

_____

American crocodile

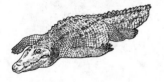

_____

rainbow trout

_____

hammerhead shark

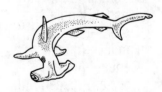

_____

California gull

_____

leopard frog

_____

leopard seal

_____

Animal Family Trees

Directions

1. Study the animal family trees shown below.
2. Cut them into 10 separate cards.
3. Find a friend and quiz each other until you can identify all of the classification groups.
4. The usual Latin names have been written in English to help you understand the system.

Kingdom—Animal
Phylum—Chordate
Class—Mammal
Order—Carnivore
Family—Cats
Genus—Big cats
Species—Lion

Kingdom—Animal
Phylum—Chordate
Class—Mammal
Order—Ungulate/having hooves
Family—Deer
Genus—Moose
Species—Moose

Kingdom—Animal
Phylum—Chordate
Class—Mammal
Order—Carnivore
Family—Hair seals
Genus—Seal
Species—Harp seal
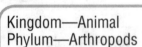

Kingdom—Animal
Phylum—Chordate
Class—Reptile
Order—Turtle
Family—Snapping Turtle Family
Genus—Turtle
Species—Snapping Turtle
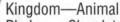

Kingdom—Animal
Phylum—Arthropods
Class—Insects
Order—Beetles
Family—Ladybug Beetles
Genus—Ladybug Beetle
Species—Nine-spotted Ladybug Beetle
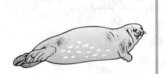

Kingdom—Animal
Phylum—Chordate
Class—Reptile
Order—Lizards and Snakes
Family—Pit Viper
Genus—Rattlesnake
Species—Timber Rattlesnake
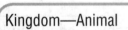

Kingdom—Animal
Phylum—Chordate
Class—Reptile
Order—Lizards
Family—Iguanid
Genus—Anole
Species—Green Anole

Kingdom—Animal
Phylum—Chordate
Class—Mammal
Order—Insectivores
Family—Shrews
Genus—Shrew
Species—Pacific Shrew

Kingdom—Animal
Phylum—Chordate
Class—Mammal
Order—Rodent
Family—Rats and Mice
Genus—Mouse
Species—Deer Mouse

Kingdom—Animal
Phylum—Chordate
Class—Amphibian
Order—Frogs and Toads
Family—True Frog
Genus—Frog
Species—Bullfrog

Collecting Scientific Names

Every living plant and animal has its own scientific name with a genus and species. The Latin scientific name and the common English name can be found in field guides that also describe and illustrate the organism.

Materials
- *notebook*
- *magnifying glass*
- *small living organisms*
- *field guides*
- *display box with plastic cover*

Directions

1. Make a collection of flowers, leaves, bark, insects, or other small living organisms. You may decide instead to draw pictures or take photos of larger animals.
2. If you make a collection, use a display box with clear plastic wrap to cover the collection.
3. Use a notebook to record each organism you find. Describe the plant or animal carefully.
4. Use field guides to identify species. You may also find Internet sites to help you.
5. Record the Latin scientific name and the common English name for each organism.
6. You may have trouble with the exact identification of all organisms. If you can tell that it is an insect or a beetle or any partial identification, use what you have.

Sample Entries

Description: black insect, very long rear legs, very long antennae, 3/4 in. long, eats plant material
Sketch:

Scientific name: (Gryllus pennsylvanicus)
Common name: Field Cricket

Description: single yellow flower, milky sap, flower turns white and blows away, leaves have triangles
Sketch:

Scientific name: (Taraxacum officinale)
Common name: Dandelion

Fish

DID YOU KNOW THAT . . . ?

● *There are about 23,000 different species of fish.*

● *The largest fish is the whale shark whose length is more than 40 feet. It weighs 16 tons, as much as two elephants.*

● *The giant sturgeon can live to be more than 100 years old.*

● *Needlefish have green bones.*

● *Sharks have cartilage instead of bones. This is the same material in human noses and ears.*

FISH FEATURES

Fish are *vertebrates* (that means they have backbones). Fish have three body parts: head, body, and tail. The head contains the eyes, mouth, and gills. Many fish have teeth in their jaws or on their tongues. The body extends from the gill covers to the tail and contains most of the fins. The tail contains the caudal fin. Fish are **cold-blooded** and cannot control their body temperature. Their bodies are the same as the temperature of the water they swim in.

FISH ADAPTATIONS

Fish come in many different shapes and sizes. They can be very small, such as tiny seahorses or as large as giant manta rays and sharks. Eels are long, ribbon-like fish. Rays and skates are flat and shaped like kites. Salmon and trout are torpedo shaped. Flatfishes are shaped like thin pancakes moving upright through the water.

Some fish living in the ocean depths can produce their own light. Cosmopolitan sailfish can swim 68 miles per hour, as fast as a car on the freeway. Lampreys attach their jaws to prey and suck blood. Gulper eels have huge unhinged jaws, so they can swallow large fish. Needlefish have very thin bodies and needle-sharp teeth. Hatchet fish have light organs along their body that can make them invisible in the ocean depths. The skin of ocean sunfish is so tough that harpoons and bullets sometimes bounce off them.

GILLS

All fish breathe in water using organs called *gills*. Oxygen is an element contained in water. Fish take in water through their mouths. The water runs over very fine layers of blood vessels in the gills where the oxygen is removed from the water and carbon dioxide is released into the water. Most fish have four pairs of gills. Oxygen travels from the gills through very thin blood vessels into the bloodstream of the fish. The water leaves the body through the gill covers.

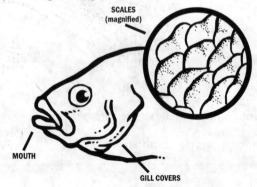

SCALES
(magnified)

MOUTH

GILL COVERS

Fish

SCALES

Fish are equipped with a natural armor. Although some fish have a tough skin, most fish are covered with scales, a series of overlapping protective plates that act like shingles or tiles on a roof. These scales protect the fish from some enemies and allow the fish to move swiftly through the water. Fish usually have thousands of scales. Fish bodies are usually slimy which makes them harder for **predators** to catch and which makes it easier to swim rapidly through the water.

FINS

Most fish have seven fins, but there are many variations among fish. Fins are made of a thin skin or membrane supported by rays or spines.

There are three single fins. The **dorsal fin** located on the top back of the fish provides balance and stability as the fish swims through the water. It varies in size and may be divided into two or three sections. The **caudal fin** (or tail fin) provides the propulsion or speed. The **anal fin** is located underneath the fish near the rear and usually just before the tail fin. There are two sets of paired fins. The two small pelvic fins help most fish to change directions and to go up or down. The pectoral fins help fish roll, change directions, and go up and down in the water.

HOW FISH SWIM

Fish have **streamlined** bodies designed to move easily through the water. Fish swim with a side-to-side movement. A fish contracts (pulls in) the muscles on one side of its body and then the other. This creates a wiggling S-shaped movement that pushes the tail fin and body against the water and drives the fish forward. The S-shaped movement begins when the fish moves its head to the right. The tail swings left and then right as the fish moves through the water. The tail fin provides the propulsion for the fish as its streamlined body slices through the water. Fish also swim up and down. Fish use their pectoral and pelvic fins to rise, stay level, or sink in the water. These fins and the dorsal fin help it to roll in the water. The dorsal fin is especially important for helping a fish keep its balance.

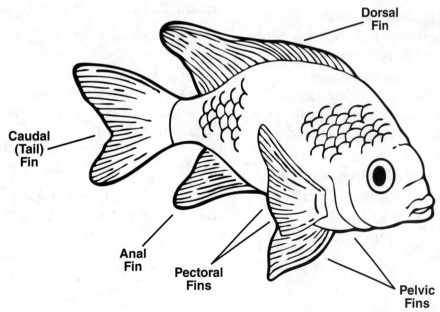

Dorsal
Fin

Caudal
(Tail)
Fin

Anal
Fin

Pectoral
Fins

Pelvic
Fins

Fish

FISH SENSES: THE LATERAL LINE

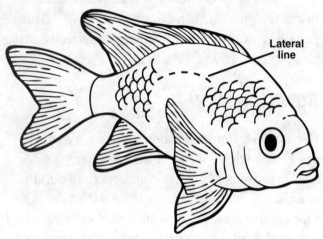

Lateral line

Fish can hear, see, smell, touch, and taste. Fish can have taste buds in their mouth and skin and even in their fins. Fish usually have a visible **lateral line** that looks like stitches along each side of the body. This line is made from smaller scales that have pores connecting to very sensitive nerve endings. The lateral line senses vibrations and helps the fish maneuver through the water and avoid predators and other dangers.

REPRODUCTION

A few fish like guppies have their babies alive. They are called live-bearers and give birth in the water. However, most fish lay eggs that hatch in the water. The newly hatched babies are called **fry**. Some fish lay only a few dozen or a hundred eggs. Others, such as the turbot and ocean sunfish, can lay millions of eggs. Most eggs and fry are on their own once the eggs are laid. However, a few fish like the seahorse keep the eggs in a pouch to protect them. The brown discus allows its babies to feed off its skin for several weeks and cichlids keep their eggs and newly hatched babies in their mouths for a month.

Facts to Remember

- *Fish are vertebrates with backbones.*

- *Fish are cold-blooded.*

- *Fish have many shapes.*

- *Fish have many **adaptations** to their environment.*

- *Fish breathe through gills.*

- *Fish have overlapping scales.*

- *Fish have seven fins which help them swim and maintain balance.*

- *Fish swim with an S-shaped movement.*

VOCABULARY

adaptations—*a creature's adjustment to its environment*

anal fin—*the fin underneath the fish*

caudal fin—*the tail fin that provides speed*

cold-blooded—*not able to regulate temperature*

dorsal fin—*the top fin on a fish*

fry—*newly hatched baby fish*

lateral line—*an organ in fish which senses vibrations*

predator—*an animal which eats other animals*

streamlined—*designed to move easily through water or air*

Goldfish

Materials
- *feeder goldfish*
- *small aquarium or fish bowl*
- *goldfish flakes*
- *bottled water*
- *magnifying glass*
- *clear, plastic cups*

(Note: Feeder goldfish can be purchased inexpensively at local pet stores.)

Directions

Place your goldfish in a clear cup of bottled water or water from the aquarium. Then study your goldfish carefully with the magnifying glass.

Eyes

Are there any eyelids? _____

Do the eyes ever close? _____

Do the eyes move? _____

Put your finger in the water at different places. Does the fish follow your finger with its eyes? _____

Place a piece of goldfish food in the water near the mouth. Did the goldfish eat the food? _____

Place a flake near the fish's tail. Did the fish find the food? _____

Fins and Features

Locate each of the seven fins on your goldfish. Use a ruler to estimate the length of each fin in millimeters. Write the estimated lengths below.

dorsal fin: _____ mm

anal fin: _____ mm

1 pectoral fin: _____ mm

caudal (tail) fin: _____ mm

1 pelvic fin: _____ mm

Illustrate each feature in the spaces below.

dorsal fin	anal fin
caudal (tail) fin	pelvic fins (2)
pectoral fins (2)	eyes (2)
mouth	gill cover
scale pattern on the body	lateral line

Guppies

Materials
- *feeder guppies*
- *small aquarium or fish bowl*
- *magnifying glass*
- *feeder goldfish*
- *bottled water*
- *clear, plastic cups*
- *fish flakes*

(Note: Feeder guppies and goldfish can be purchased inexpensively at local pet stores.)

Directions

1. Place your guppy in a clear cup of bottled water or water from the aquarium.
2. Study your guppy carefully with the magnifying glass.
3. Describe the colors of your guppy. Look for different flecks of color.

   _____

4. Place a fish flake in the water. How did your guppy react to the food?

   _____

5. Draw a sketch of your guppy on a separate sheet of paper. Label the following features: eyes, gill covers, dorsal fin, pectoral fins, pelvic fins, anal fin, and caudal (tail) fin.

Goldfish and Guppy—Alike and Different

Place a goldfish in your cup. Compare the two fish. Tell what is alike and different about each fish in the categories listed below.

Size: _____

_____

Fins: _____

_____

Eyes: _____

_____

Shape: _____

_____

Mouth: _____

_____

Behavior in the water: _____

_____

Colors: _____

_____

Draw sketches here to illustrate your comparisons.

Guppy Sketch	Goldfish Sketch

Student Inquiry Activity

Spend some time watching guppies and goldfish in an aquarium. Watch how they move and swim. Look at their physical features—eyes, gills, lateral line, fins, and mouth. Look at the patterns of color and arrangement on the scales.

Observations

Write down any observations that you find interesting.

1. _____
2. _____
3. _____
4. _____
5. _____
6. _____

Inquiry Questions

Write down any questions about fish that you might be able to answer in an inquiry investigation.

1. _____
2. _____
3. _____

Suggested Inquiry Investigations

- How are any two fish alike, and how are they different in behavior and physical features?

- How are fish and tadpoles alike, and how do they differ?

- What are the similarities and differences between fish and mammals?

- What foods eaten by people or pets will fish eat?

- How does the water in an aquarium change in color and quality from day to day?

- What other aquarium fish will live with guppies and goldfish?

- Can you get any fish to reproduce by laying eggs or having live babies?

- How does the fish use its lateral line and eyes to avoid obstacles?

Getting Started

Select one of your ideas or one of the suggested topics to use for an inquiry investigation. Collect your materials. Make sure to get approval from your parents and teacher. Use the Student Inquiry Worksheets to complete the activity.

Your Inquiry Choice: _____

_____

Materials you will need: _____

_____

Insects

DID YOU KNOW THAT . . . ?

- There are probably more than 200 million insects in the world for each human being.

- Some mayflies live only a few hours.

- Cicadas can be heard a quarter of a mile away.

- The American cockroach is the fastest running insect. It can run about three miles an hour for short distances.

- One termite queen may lay over 400,000,000 eggs in her lifetime.

ARTHROPODS

There are about one million known insect species but there may be as many as 30 million more species to be discovered. Insects make up about 85 percent of all animal species. Insects are part of a larger group of invertebrates (animals without backbones) called *arthropods*. They have a tough, hard outer body covering, legs with joints, a nerve cord down the length of the body, and a segmented body. Arthropods include arachnids (spiders and their relatives), crustaceans (crabs, lobsters, and millipedes), scorpions, as well as insects.

INSECT SPECIES

Insects have adapted to live in almost every climate on Earth and in very different conditions. They live in tropical heat at the equator and in the extreme cold of the polar regions. They live in forests, deserts, mountains, rain forests, rivers, oceans, and even in the most polluted habitats.

There are 32 orders (groups of related species) of insects. These include over 300,000 species of beetles. Beetles have hard outer wings covering softer inner wings. There are almost 100,000 species of flies, mosquitoes, and gnats. These insects have only two wings, unlike most insects that usually have four wings. There are more than 130,000 species of butterflies and moths. These insects have wings covered with many small, soft scales.

Crickets and grasshoppers have very strong rear legs designed for jumping and straight wings. There are 20,000 species of crickets and grasshoppers. There are more than 110,000 species of ants, bees, and wasps which have two wings on each side of the body that hook together to work like a single wing. There are 5,000 species of dragonflies and damselflies that usually hunt for other insects over ponds and lakes.

Insects

INSECT FEATURE: HEAD

Insects have three distinct body parts: head, **thorax**, and **abdomen**. The head has two antennae used to help insects feel their way through their environment. These antennae are used for tasting and smelling, as well as touching. Adult insects have two compound eyes on the head that have many light sensitive parts. The compound eyes have hundreds of individual lenses. They see many facets (separate parts of a picture—somewhat like a broken mirror). Insects also have one to three simple eyes which only sense light. The **mandibles** are a pair of jaws that move from side to side. Insects use the mandibles located on their head for chewing, grasping prey, and eating. An insect's brain is located in its head.

INSECT FEATURE: THORAX

The middle section of the insect is the *thorax*. The thorax has three separate segments with one pair of legs attached to each segment of the thorax. Insects have no veins or arteries. Blood flows freely through their bodies. Insects take in air through holes along the side of the body. These are called **spiracles**. There is usually one pair of spiracles on each body segment with a hole on each side of the body. Air travels directly to the muscles and organs that need oxygen just like other animals.

INSECT FEATURE: ABDOMEN

The abdomen is shaped like a tube and usually has about 11 segments. The abdomen contains most of the heart and digestive systems. The reproductive organs are located there as well. The female usually has an egg-laying organ called an **ovipositor** that extends from the rear of the body.

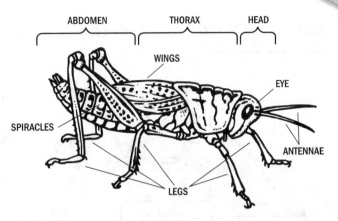

The wings often extend beyond the rear of the abdomen. If the insect is poisonous, the poison glands are located in the abdomen. Many insects have a pair of **cerci** extending from the rear of the last abdominal segment. Each cercus is used for sensing like a rear antenna.

INSECT FEATURE: WINGS

Most insects have wings at some time in their lives, but they vary greatly in use, location, and style. The wings are attached to the thorax. Hard, protective curved outer wings cover beetles. These wings provide lift while thin, soft underwings provide the thrust or forward motion of the beetles. Some insects, like bees and wasps, have thin, membrane-like wings. Damselflies, dragonflies, and mayflies have thin, translucent membrane-like wings as well. Some dragonflies can fly at speeds of 35 miles an hour, as fast as cars on a city street. Most insects have four wings, but flies only have two wings. Flies can use these wings to hover or to reverse directions and fly backwards.

Unit 4

Insects

INSECT LIFE CYCLE: COMPLETE METAMORPHOSIS

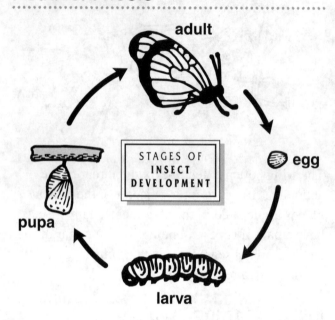

STAGES OF INSECT DEVELOPMENT

adult

egg

larva

pupa

Most insects go through four stages of development called complete **metamorphosis** (change). These include insects like mealworms and other beetles like the ladybug, butterflies, and moths. These insects lay eggs either attached to plants that will provide food when the egg hatches or in locations where food is immediately available.

EGGS AND LARVAE

The eggs hatch into larvae that eat until their bodies stretch tight. Since the hard outer skin, the **exoskeleton**, cannot stretch or expand, the larva stops eating and **molts**. It bursts through the skin and forms a newer, softer, looser skin. Because larvae are basically eating machines that do little but eat and rest, they soon outgrow the new skin and molt again. The stages between molts are called **instars**, and the larva will go through several instars before it enters the next stage of its life cycle. Larvae look like worms and usually have 13 segments.

PUPA

After the larva has reached its final instar, it will stop eating, rest, and eventually change into a pupa. Butterflies and beetles do not spin cocoons, but some moths do. These moths spin a cocoon made of silk or a combination of silk and leaves to form a protective case for the pupa before it emerges as an adult. The pupas of other insects form a hard protective cover and attach themselves to a tree, a leaf, or stem and go through several days of immobility while their body changes to the adult insect. They often appear dead or look like leaf parts.

ADULT

When the pupa has been transformed inside the casing of the **chrysalis** or the cocoon, the adult breaks open a spot on the chrysalis and pushes its way out. Moths emerging from a cocoon secrete an acid that eats its way through the cocoon and allows the new moth to slide out. Adult moths and butterflies flap their wings slowly for a short time pumping blood into the veins of the wings. The wings soon become stiff and the moth or butterfly is ready to fly off in search of a mate.

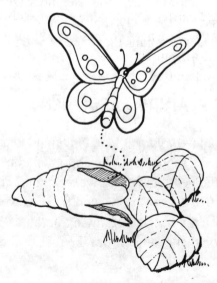

Insects

INCOMPLETE METAMORPHOSIS

Crickets, locusts, and grasshoppers are good examples of insects that go through only three stages of development in a process called incomplete metamorphosis: egg, **nymph**, and adult. The changes are not nearly as dramatic in these insects as in those that go through complete metamorphosis. Eggs are laid in areas where food will be available to the insect when it hatches. The egg hatches into a nymph that is smaller in size and resembles the adult insect but does not yet have wings. It may also be lighter in color. As the insect molts and sheds its skin several times, the wings develop, the insect grows, and the adult finally develops.

BENEFITS AND PROBLEMS FOR MAN

Some insects are very important to people. Bees and wasps help pollinate many flowers and are essential to some plant reproduction. Bees produce honey which has always been a food favored by humans. Flies also help in pollination. Silkworms are raised to produce cocoons that are used in making silk cloth. Ladybugs eat many insects, such as aphids and scale insects that harm flowers and other crops. Fleas and flies are disease carriers that spread contagious and dangerous organisms to humans and domesticated animals. Mosquito bites can cause malaria. Human and animal lice can spread disease as well.

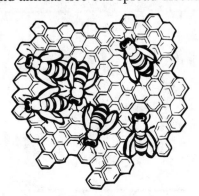

Facts to Remember

- *Insects belong to the larger group of invertebrates called arthropods.*
- *Insects live in almost all climates and conditions on Earth.*
- *There are over one million known species of insects.*
- *Insects have three main body parts: head, thorax, and abdomen.*
- *Insects have six legs and most have four wings.*
- *Most insects go through four stages of insect development in complete metamorphosis: egg, larva, pupa, and adult.*
- *Some insects go through three stages of insect development in incomplete metamorphosis: egg, nymph, and adult.*

VOCABULARY

abdomen—*the rear section of an insect body*

cercus (cerci)—*rear feelers on an insect*

chrysalis—*the cocoon stage of an insect*

exoskeleton—*hard outer skin*

instars—*larval stages; molts*

mandibles—*insect jaws*

metamorphosis—*change*

molt—*shedding of the exoskeleton by the larva*

nymph—*a middle stage of insect growth*

ovipositor—*insect egg layer*

spiracles—*air holes in an insect body*

thorax—*the middle section of an insect*

Keeping an Insect Vivarium

Materials
- *assorted, collected insects*
- *plastic or glass jar or old aquarium*
- *fine mesh screening or nylon stocking and large rubber band*
- *water sprayer*
- *soft dirt or potting soil*
- *wet paper towel*
- *egg carton piece or small box*
- *dead leaves, sticks, grass, stones*
- *sod*
- *apple slice, oatmeal, chicken starter mash, breadcrumbs, carrot*

Directions

1. Cover the bottom of your plastic container, glass jar, or aquarium with one or two inches of soft dirt or potting soil.
2. Scatter a variety of dead leaves, sticks, and grass around the vivarium. Add a few small stones.
3. Plant a few clumps of sod (grass with roots) in the dirt.
4. Place a jar cover or small plastic cup with an apple slice, oatmeal, chicken starter mash, breadcrumbs, a raw carrot or similar foods in the container. Change the foods when they get hard or start to spoil or mold.
5. Fold a small wad of wet paper towel and place it in a corner.
6. Use a sprayer to keep the leaves, plants, and dirt damp.
7. Place a small piece of egg carton or small box for insects to hide in the vivarium.
8. Place your insects in the vivarium.
9. Cover the vivarium with screening or a nylon stocking held on with a large rubber band.

Recording Observations

List the insects you have placed in your vivarium. Then sketch and describe each insect. Describe each insect's behavior including where each insect lives, what it eats, and what it does.

Insect name: _____   Sketch

Description: _____

_____

Behavior: _____

_____

_____

Insect name: _____   Sketch

Description: _____

_____

Behavior: _____

_____

_____

Crickets

Materials
- *cricket*
- *magnifying glass*
- *sliced apples or potatoes*
- *insect vivarium*
- *ruler*
- *chicken starter mash, apple and potato slices*
- *clear plastic cups*
- *pencil*

(Note: You can purchase crickets inexpensively in pet stores. They can be kept in an insect vivarium as described on page 44.)

Cricket Features

Place one cricket in a clear, plastic cup. Use a magnifying glass to examine its features and a metric ruler to measure it. Answer these questions.

How many legs can you count? _____

Which pair of legs is the longest? _____

To which part of the body are the legs attached? _____

How long are the front legs? _____ mm

How long are the middle pair of legs? _____ mm

How long are the rear legs? _____ mm

How many wings does the cricket have? _____

Which antenna is longer—the left or right? _____

How long is the longest antenna? _____ mm

How long are the two rear cerci (feelers) extending from the rear of the body? _____ mm

Sketches

Draw a sketch of your cricket from the top. Label these features: eyes, antennae, legs, head, thorax, abdomen, wings, and cerci.

Draw a sketch of your cricket showing the underside of the insect. Label as many features as you can.

Cricket Behavior

Put your finger or a pencil near the head of the cricket. How does it react? _____

Put a finger or a pencil near the rear of the cricket. How does it react? _____

What foods have you seen the cricket eat? _____

Will it eat sliced apple, sliced raw potato, or chicken starter mash? _____

Does the cricket like the light or dark? _____

Ladybugs

Materials
- *ladybugs*
- *magnifying glass*
- *grass stems, leaves, twigs*
- *clear, plastic cup or plastic, sandwich bag*
- *insect vivarium (see page 44)*
- *index card*
- *rubber band*

(Note: Ladybugs can be purchased inexpensively in garden stores.)

Investigating Ladybugs

1. Put one or more ladybugs in a clear, plastic cup or plastic, sandwich bag.
2. Cover the cup with an index card, paper, or plastic, sandwich bag held in place by a rubber band.
3. Use a magnifying glass to study the ladybug.
4. How many spots does your ladybug have? _____
5. Look at the hard outer wings. Can you see the thinner underwings beneath the outer wings? _____
6. Does your ladybug move in the jar? _____
7. Which direction does it usually move? _____

Sketching Ladybugs

Carefully examine the features of your ladybug. Then draw a detailed sketch of your ladybug below. Label the following features: eye, elytra (outer wings), head, thorax, abdomen, legs, mouth, antennae, and underwings.

Draw a sketch of the underside of your ladybug. Then label the features that are visible underneath.

Ladybug Activities

- Place some grass stems or thin twigs and a leaf in the plastic cup with the ladybug or in your insect vivarium.
- Observe your ladybug's movements and activities.
- Describe where your ladybug goes, how it moves, and what it does.

_____

_____

_____

Student Inquiry Activity

You have studied ladybug features and behaviors. What scientific information would you like to know about ladybugs? Use the Student Inquiry Worksheets to design and plan your inquiry investigation.

Inquiry Investigation: Sample Ideas

- What insects will ladybugs eat?
- How do ladybugs rest or sleep?
- What areas of the insect vivarium do ladybugs prefer?
- Do ladybugs prefer wet or dry areas?
- How strong are the outer wings of a ladybug?
- How do ladybugs act when they meet other ladybugs?
- Do ladybugs prefer the dark, soft light, or bright light?
- Do ladybugs like the warmth or cold?
- Can ladybugs swim?
- Do ladybugs prefer high or low areas in a container?
- How do ladybugs play possum (act dead)?
- When do ladybugs leak blood (orange)?

Brainstorming: Ladybug Ideas to Investigate

Write some ideas of your own that you would like to test about ladybugs during an investigation. List all of your own ideas as fast as they come to mind.

1. _____
2. _____
3. _____
4. _____

Eliminate Some Ideas

- Eliminate any idea that is unsafe for you or the ladybug.
- Eliminate any idea that cannot be tested.
- Eliminate any idea that may not teach you anything.

Your Decision

Choose one of your ideas or one of the suggestions listed at the top of the page. Write your choice on the line below and tell why you chose that idea.

Your Inquiry Investigation: _____

_____

I chose this inquiry investigation because . . . _____

_____

Do It

Design the inquiry, do the investigation, and record your results.

Student Inquiry Activity

Use the Student Inquiry Worksheets to design and plan your inquiry investigation.

Inquiry Questions about Butterflies and Moths

Consider these questions about butterflies and moths.
- How can I tell a butterfly from a moth?
- How can I find and raise butterfly or moth eggs found in gardens or other natural settings?
- What will I learn from hatching butterflies or moths from eggs, such as painted lady butterflies, purchased from nature stores?
- Can I grow moths from pupas and cocoons found in gardens, vacant lots, or other natural settings?
- Can I raise butterflies or moths from caterpillars found in gardens, trees, and empty lots?
- What foods do butterflies and moths eat?

Notes to Remember

- Always bring several leaves and other plant materials from the same place where eggs, caterpillars, pupas, and adult moths and butterflies are found.
- Keep all of your living materials in an insect vivarium.
- Regularly observe specimens to see what they are eating or doing and to anticipate insect food needs.

I Know

List four things you can think of that you learned about insects, especially butterflies and moths, now that you have done the reading and activities in this unit.

1. _____
2. _____
3. _____
4. _____

What You Don't Know

Think of all the things you don't know about butterflies and moths that you could discover. Write down three inquiry questions you could ask about butterflies and moths and the answers you hope to find conducting an investigation.

Inquiry #1: _____

Inquiry #2: _____

Inquiry #3: _____

Making Decisions and Getting Started

Choose an inquiry question from your own list or those at the top of the page. Base your choice on what interests you and what you can hope to learn.

Your Inquiry Choice: _____

_____

What do you have to do to get started? _____

_____

Human Body

DID YOU KNOW THAT . . . ?

- *The oldest complete human corpse was found in the Alps. The body, nicknamed "The Iceman," was over 5,000 years old.*

- *Some human body cells last only a few days. A brain cell can last for life.*

- *All of the nerves in the human body laid end to end would stretch over 45 miles.*

- *Eyelids can blink five times a second.*

- *The human heart will beat about two billion times in an average lifetime.*

- *Humans use more than 200 different muscles to walk.*

- *Babies have about 300 bones at birth. Many fuse together during the process of growing up.*

- *The human brain contains about 15 billion cells.*

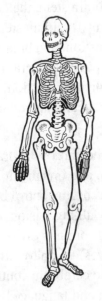

THE SKELETON

The framework of bones in the human body is called the *skeleton*. These bones support the body and protect sensitive internal organs, such as the brain, heart, liver, and lungs. Muscles are attached to bones. The spinal cord is the main framework of bones that supports the body. The spine is formed by many small bones called *vertebrae* or *ribs*. A baby's skeleton is flexible. The bones harden as humans age.

BONES

There are 206 bones in the average human body. The longest bone is the thigh bone in the leg. Long bones have a hard outer layer that covers an inner layer of tissue called *marrow*. Red and white blood cells are constantly produced by **bone marrow**. Red blood cells last about four months before they are replaced. Fat is also stored in bone marrow. Bones have calcium and phosphorous in them which make them hard. Bones meet at joints that are held together by strong bonds called *ligaments*. These joints allow the muscles to move freely. The joints are lined with lubricating fluids to prevent pain and wear on the bones. The skull is extremely hard. It protects the brain from stress and damage. Many of the smaller bones are in the hands and feet.

Human Body

BRAIN

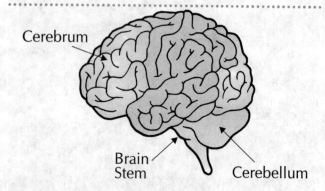

Cerebrum

Brain
Stem

Cerebellum

An adult human brain weighs about three pounds. It is the most important organ of the nervous system. The brain is constantly sending and receiving messages in the form of electrical impulses through the central nervous system. The brain is the control center for all of the functions of the human body. There are three main sections of the brain: the brain stem, the **cerebellum**, and the **cerebrum**. The brain stem controls the heartbeat, digestion, and breathing. The cerebellum is the part of the brain that controls balance and muscle coordination. Both of these areas work automatically and do not require thinking.

The cerebrum is the part of the brain that controls thinking, memory, and imagination. Various sections of the cerebrum control basic voluntary movements, like walking, vision, hearing, speech, and emotions. The brain is divided into two hemispheres (halves) that have different functions. The left side of the cerebrum controls speech, thought, numbers, and language, while the right side of the brain controls imagination, music, art, and similar creative activities.

NERVOUS SYSTEM

The nervous system is made up of the brain, the spinal cord, and an extensive system of nerves that extend into every area of the human body. Nerve cells carry messages to and from the brain along the spinal cord and the nerves. There are billions of nerve cells in the body. If all the nerves in the body were laid end-to-end, they would make a thin line nearly 50 miles long.

THE CIRCULATORY SYSTEM: HEART AND BLOOD

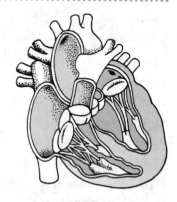

The human heart is a muscle the size of a fist and weighs about three pounds. The heart pumps blood throughout the body. There are two sides of the heart: the left and the right. Each side also has two sections called an *atrium* and a *ventricle*. The stronger left side pumps blood filled with oxygen from the lungs to the rest of the body along blood vessels called **arteries**. The weaker right side brings blood back to the lungs along blood vessels called **veins** to receive more oxygen. Human blood is a very complex fluid that contains red blood cells for carrying oxygen, white blood cells to fight off infection, and platelets to help blood clot when we bleed. The heart, blood, and blood vessels make up the circulatory system of the human body.

Human Body

LUNGS AND THE RESPIRATORY SYSTEM

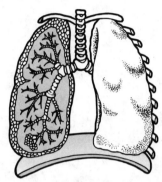

Lungs are the only organ of the human body light enough to float on water. We breathe air in through the nose, mouth, and windpipe (in the throat). The air flows through two bronchial tubes and into tiny hollow tubes called *alveoli* located in the lungs. There are more than 700 million of these microscopic alveoli in the lungs. They are covered with tiny **capillary** arteries and veins. Blood going through these small tubes gives off carbon dioxide, a waste product of breathing, and picks up oxygen, essential to life. The base of each lung rests on the diaphragm, a muscle that pulls down on the lungs when we inhale bringing air into the trachea (windpipe). The lungs contract and force air out when we exhale.

TEETH

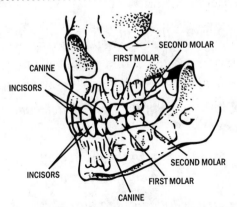

Young children have a set of 20 temporary teeth. These begin to fall out at age six and are followed

by a set of 32 permanent teeth. Human teeth have a very hard enamel covering. The pulp contains blood vessels that allow teeth to grow and live. Strong fibers hold the teeth in place in the jaw. The 12 front teeth contain incisors and canine teeth used to hold and tear food. The back 20 teeth are molars and premolars which are used for grinding and chewing food. When chewing, the jaw is pulled upward by powerful muscles.

THE DIGESTIVE SYSTEM: MOUTH AND STOMACH

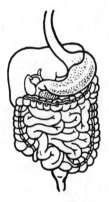

The digestive tract is a series of connected tubes about 30 feet long winding and coiling through the body. Digestion starts in the mouth when food is chewed, and saliva in the mouth adds chemicals that start to break down the food. The tongue rolls the food to the back of the throat where it is swallowed down the food pipe called the esophagus to the stomach. Acidic juices and other chemicals break down the food in the stomach into a soup-like liquid.

Human Body

THE DIGESTIVE SYSTEM: SMALL AND LARGE INTESTINE

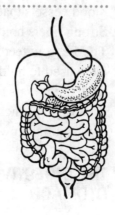

A ball at one end of the stomach called the *duodenum* receives bile from the liver and chemical juices from the pancreas that help to further break down food. As food moves into the small intestine, many of the chemical substances are absorbed into the blood. Water and tough fibers which are left are moved to the large intestine where bacteria breaks down the tough remaining leftovers, and a lot of the water is absorbed into the body. The left over undigested material is then expelled from the body. Kidneys clean unwanted substances out of the blood by filtering out wastes. This material is expelled from the body in the form of urine.

MUSCLES

Muscles are essential to movement. More than 600 muscles make up more than half the weight of a human body. Muscles contract when triggered by messages carried by the nerves. Voluntary muscles are controlled by the person. Involuntary muscles are not controlled and handle many internal functions, such as digestion.

SKIN

Skin is the largest organ of the human body. There are two main layers of skin that total about two millimeters thick. The skin has nerve cells that react to sensations, such as pressure, heat, cold, and pain. Skin is constantly being shed in very small particles. Hair and nails are extensions of skin made of a substance called *keratin*. Hair and skin have no nerve cells and thus lack feeling.

Facts to Remember

● *The skeleton is the framework of bones supporting the body.*

● *There are 206 bones in the average adult human.*

● *Blood cells are produced by bone marrow.*

● *There are three major parts to the human brain: brain stem, cerebellum, and cerebrum.*

● *Nerve cells carry messages to and from the brain along the spinal cord.*

● *The heart pumps blood through blood vessels through the body.*

● *Blood going through the lungs picks up oxygen and gives off carbon dioxide.*

● *Digestion starts in the mouth and is completed in the small intestine.*

VOCABULARY

artery—*carries blood with oxygen to the rest of the body*

bone marrow—*tissue in larger bones which makes blood cells*

capillary—*very small blood vessel*

cerebellum—*part of the brain which controls balance*

cerebrum—*the part of the brain controlling thought, speech, memory, and vision*

vein—*carries blood back to the heart*

How Does Your Heart Beat?

Materials
clock or watch

Directions

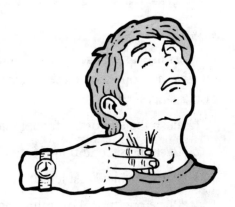

1. Do this activity with a friend or classmate.
2. Use your index and middle fingers to find your carotid artery on the left side of your neck. You should be able to feel a regular movement or beat against your fingers. This is called a *pulse*.
3. Then find the carotid artery on your friend's neck.
4. Have your friend monitor the time for one minute, while you count the heartbeats at this artery.
5. Record the pulse (heartbeat).
   First Team Member's Pulse: _____
6. Measure the other person's heartbeat and record the pulse.
   Second Team Member's Pulse: _____

Exercise Your Heart

1. The first team member should run in place, do jumping jacks, or do some exercise for two minutes.
2. Take the pulse of the first team member immediately after the exercise.
   First Team Member's Pulse After Exercise: _____
3. Have the second team member exercise in the same way.
4. Take the pulse of the second team member immediately after the exercise.
   Second Team Member's Pulse After Exercise: _____

   Did exercise affect the pulse rate? _____

Try This

Most nurses use the wrist to record the pulse. The wrist pulse is sometimes harder to find in children. Study the illustration to the right. Use the index and middle fingers to find your partner's pulse. (Do not use the thumb. It has a pulse of its own which would distort the count.)

First Team Member's Wrist Pulse: _____

Second Team Member's Wrist Pulse: _____

Were the pulse counts the same or different as those done with the carotid artery? _____

_____

Which count did you think was more accurate? Why? _____

_____

Hearing Heartbeats

Materials
- *clock or watch*
- *metal or plastic funnels*
- *a foot of plastic tubing*
- *paper towel tube*
- *tube made from tagboard*

Directions

Doctors use a stethoscope to monitor heartbeats. You can make your own stethoscope with these materials. Do this activity with a friend or classmate.

1. Push the end of the funnel into one end of the plastic tube.

2. Push the second funnel into the other end of the tubing.

3. Put your hand just left of the center of the chest.

4. Place one funnel over this spot where the heart is located.

5. The other partner should listen through the second funnel for the heartbeat that will be heard as a thump-thump, two-stroke sound.

6. Keep adjusting the funnel over your heart until your partner can clearly hear the beat.

Counting Beats

1. Keep time for one minute while your partner counts each two-beat sound as one beat.

2. Record your heartbeat. _____

3. Switch partners and adjust the stethoscope until you hear your partner's heartbeat.

4. Record your partner's heartbeat. _____

Try This

1. Use a paper towel tube, a wrapping paper tube, or a tube made from tag board as a stethoscope.

2. Carefully locate the tube over the heart until you can hear the two-stroke beat.

3. Record the results.

    First Partner's Heartbeat: _____
    Second Partner's Heartbeat: _____

Fingerprints

Materials
• *inkpad*   • *paper towel*   • *magnifying glass*

Directions

No two human beings have the same fingerprints or tongue prints. Fingerprint patterns can vary greatly among individuals. Follow the directions below.

1. Make sure the inkpad is damp with ink.
2. Ink one fingertip at a time.
3. Carefully place the finger in the proper box and roll it so that the print is clear and complete in the square.
4. Clean your fingers with a paper towel.

Left Hand

Little Finger	Ring Finger	Middle Finger	Index Finger	Thumb

Right Hand

Little Finger	Ring Finger	Middle Finger	Index Finger	Thumb

Patterns

All fingerprints have these three shapes in common (see below).

Whorl   **Loop**   **Arch**

1. Use a magnifying glass to study each fingerprint.
2. Label each of your 10 prints above as whorl, loop, or arch on the chart below. Make your best judgment about those in which you are uncertain.
3. Compare your fingerprints with those of a classmate. Write your classmate's pattern below.
4. Then compare patterns with other classmates.
5. Can you find a classmate with the same pattern on one or both hands? _____

Left-Hand Pattern

	LF	RF	MF	IF	T
You					
1st					
2nd					

Right-Hand Pattern

	LF	RF	MF	IF	T
You					
1st					
2nd					

Student Inquiry Activity

Use the Student Inquiry Worksheets to design and plan your inquiry investigation.

Inquiry Questions to Consider

Breathing
- How many breaths does an average fifth grader take in one minute?
- How many breaths does an adult take in one minute?
- What is the breathing rate for children younger than you?

Heartbeat
- What is the average pulse rate for fifth graders?
- What is the most effective stethoscope you can make?
- What is the average pulse rate for girls?
- What is the average pulse rate for boys?
- What is the average pulse rate for fifth graders after exercising for 10 minutes?

Senses: Touch, Smell, Hearing
- What substances can you identify blindfolded by touch alone?
- Which finger tip is the most sensitive?
- Which sounds can you identify by hearing alone?
- Which substances can you identify by smell alone?

Other Human Features
- Can you identify separate styles of toe prints?
- Do people have individual toe prints that are distinctive only to them?
- How many different types of hair are there in one class?
- How many different blood types can you find? Are some blood types more common than others?

Making Choices

Choose three of the topics above or similar ideas that interest you. Tell why they appeal to you and what you would have to do to conduct the inquiry.

Inquiry #1: _____

It is interesting because . . . _____

_____

To do the inquiry, I would have to . . . _____

_____

Inquiry #2: _____

It is interesting because . . . _____

_____

To do the inquiry, I would have to . . . _____

_____

Inquiry #3: _____

It is interesting because . . . _____

_____

To do the inquiry, I would have to . . . _____

_____

Weather

DID YOU KNOW THAT . . . ?

- *There are more than 140,000,000,000,000 (140 trillion) tons of water vapor in the atmosphere above Earth at any given time.*

- *On average, water vapor stays in the air about 10 days before it falls as rain or snow.*

- *The total amount of rain, snow, and other precipitation is about 5,000,000,000,000,000 (5 quadrillion) tons a year.*

WEATHER IN A NUTSHELL

Weather is the combination of changing conditions in the lowest layer of the atmosphere called the *troposphere* that extends about six miles into the sky. Weather in any given location and time depends on four main elements. These are wind, moisture, **air pressure**, and **temperature**. Aspects of weather include the amount of **precipitation** (rain and snow), the hours of sunshine, atmospheric pressure, humidity (the amount of water vapor in the air), and cloud formations, as well as wind speed and direction.

IT STARTS WITH THE SUN

Weather is primarily created by the Sun's heat and the effect of that heat on the atmosphere. Heat causes water to evaporate, especially along the vast layers of water in the ocean. This **evaporation** creates clouds of water vapor. These clouds eventually produce rain or snow. The Sun's heat warms air that rises creating areas of low and high pressure. **Wind** is the movement of air from high-pressure areas to low-pressure areas.

ONE GIANT SYSTEM

Although most people think of weather as a local event, all of the weather on Earth is really a part of an interconnected system. The Sun's heat starts the system, but the world ocean covering 71% of the Earth's surface is the giant cauldron which fuels weather patterns throughout the world. The great movements of wind and water begin over the oceans. Small changes of temperature in the middle of the Pacific Ocean can impact the weather over entire continents. **Climate** is the average weather of an area over long periods of time. It changes more gradually than weather events, but it is eventually changed by events in the oceans. Deserts expand, glaciers melt, and rainforests become smaller due to long term weather patterns in the oceans.

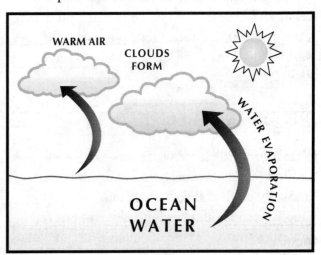

Unit 6

Weather

SUNSHINE AND TEMPERATURE

Energy from the Sun reaches Earth as light and heat. One of the first indicators of weather that people notice is sunshine. They often judge the weather by the intensity of the sunshine even on cold days. Temperature is probably the first concern people have about the weather. Temperature is measured with thermometers using either of two scales. The Fahrenheit scale is usually used in the United States to record and report weather. It is based on a scale with 32°F as the freezing point of water and 212°F as the boiling point of water. Temperatures between 32°F and 60°F are cold or cool. Those between 70°F and 100°F are warm or hot. Scientists measure temperature on the Celsius scale where 0°C is the freezing point of water and 100°C is the boiling point of water. A warm, mild day on the Celsius scale would be about 21°C.

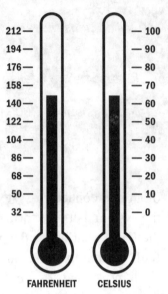

FAHRENHEIT   CELSIUS

CLOUDS AND PRECIPITATION

Clouds form when the water vapor in warm air rises into the atmosphere. This warm air gradually cools and condenses into water droplets. Clouds keep building as long as warm wet air continues to rise. There are many types of clouds that are classified according to their shapes and height above the ground. Clouds release their moisture as rain or snow or other precipitation.

WIND

Wind is the movement of air throughout the atmosphere. Air moves in patterns based on areas of low and high pressure. Wind direction is affected by the rotation of Earth as well. Wind can be extremely damaging to human lives and property. It can also be harnessed to provide clean energy.

Facts to Remember

● *Weather is produced by changes in the lowest level of the atmosphere.*

● *There are four main elements of weather: wind, moisture, air pressure, and temperature.*

● *Weather is strongly affected by heat from the Sun.*

● *Oceans generate much of the weather over continents due to evaporation and changes of water temperature.*

● *Temperature is measured on two scales: Fahrenheit and Celsius.*

VOCABULARY

air pressure—*the weight or gravitational pull of the air*

climate—*weather in a region over a long period of time*

evaporation—*formation of water vapor caused by the Sun's heat*

precipitation—*rain and snow*

temperature—*the hotness or coldness of the air*

wind—*movement of air from high pressure areas to low pressure*

Comparing Temperatures

Materials
- *thermometer*
- *Internet*
- *almanac*
- *newspaper/TV/radio*

Questions to Ask
- Is the temperature at your home and school the same as the recorded temperature for your community or city?
- Are reported temperatures in your community higher or lower than last year for the same time?
- How do your temperatures compare to those in another city where your friends or other members of your family live?
- What is the temperature for the same days in another country which you would like to visit someday?

Directions
1. Use a thermometer to measure the temperature at your home or school, then record the temperature at your home or school on the chart below.
2. Use Internet, radio, newspaper, or television sources to find the recorded high and low daily temperature for your community, another city, and a city in another country.
3. Compare the four temperatures and describe the similarities and differences with your home or school on a separate sheet of paper.

Date	Your Home/School (High/Low)	Your City (High/Low)	Another City (High/Low)	Another Country (High/Low)
	_____ / _____	_____ / _____	_____ / _____	_____ / _____
	_____ / _____	_____ / _____	_____ / _____	_____ / _____
	_____ / _____	_____ / _____	_____ / _____	_____ / _____
	_____ / _____	_____ / _____	_____ / _____	_____ / _____
	_____ / _____	_____ / _____	_____ / _____	_____ / _____
	_____ / _____	_____ / _____	_____ / _____	_____ / _____
	_____ / _____	_____ / _____	_____ / _____	_____ / _____

What temperature patterns did you notice? _____

_____

Compare your local temperatures to those recorded for last year.

Keeping a Weather Journal

Directions

Use this chart to record the weather on a five-day journal. Record both the morning and afternoon weather.

1. Record whether the sun was shining brightly or whether it was overcast and dark.
2. Record the temperature.
3. Record whether the wind was blowing. Indicate whether it was still, breezy, or very windy. Describe the wind.
4. Describe the clouds.
5. Record whether there was any precipitation in the form of rain or snow. Describe whether it was light or heavy.

Day 1	Morning	Afternoon
Sunshine		
Temperature		
Wind		
Clouds		
Rain/Snow		

Day 2	Morning	Afternoon
Sunshine		
Temperature		
Wind		
Clouds		
Rain/Snow		

Day 3	Morning	Afternoon
Sunshine		
Temperature		
Wind		
Clouds		
Rain/Snow		

Day 4	Morning	Afternoon
Sunshine		
Temperature		
Wind		
Clouds		
Rain/Snow		

Day 5	Morning	Afternoon
Sunshine		
Temperature		
Wind		
Clouds		
Rain/Snow		

Wind

DID YOU KNOW THAT . . . ?

- *There are two **jet streams** (one in each hemisphere) several hundred miles wide which circle the earth about six miles above the ground.*

- *The polar jet stream in the Northern Hemisphere can reach speeds of 250 miles per hour.*

- *The highest wind speed ever recorded on the surface of Earth was at Mount Washington, New Hampshire on April 12, 1934. The speed was 231 miles per hour.*

WIND AND AIR PRESSURE

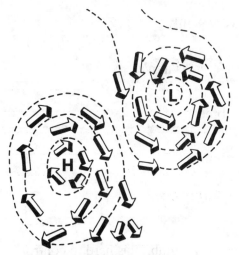

Air never stops moving. The constant circulation of air between areas of different temperature and air pressure creates wind. Wind carries heat and moisture throughout the world. Wind is dependent upon several factors. **Atmospheric pressure** and temperature create wind. Air moves from areas of high atmospheric pressure to areas of low pressure. Cold air is heavier and sinks creating areas of high pressure. These are called "**highs**." This sinking air absorbs moisture in the air and often signals light winds and clear skies with no **precipitation** (rain or snow). Warm air is lighter and rises into the atmosphere. This creates areas of low pressure called "**lows**" or "depressions." This rising warm air forms clouds and may bring wet weather.

Areas near oceans and seas often have local land and sea breezes created by the warming and cooling of air over land and water. Land heats up and cools down more quickly than water, and the cool air sinks and flows out to the sea at night and in from the sea during the day.

PREVAILING WINDS

Some winds blow all the time in the same place. They are called **prevailing winds**. These winds affect weather all over Earth. They are generated because the direct rays of the Sun heat the air at the **equator** more than the air at Earth's North and South poles. Hot air then moves north and south from the equator. Cooler air moves in to take the place of the warm air.

THE CORIOLIS EFFECT

The rotation of Earth spinning on its axis changes the direction of wind. Earth spins from west to east. This rotation of Earth deflects winds to the right in the Northern Hemisphere (above the equator) and to the left in the Southern Hemisphere (below the equator). This is called the **Coriolis Effect**. There is little wind movement along the equator itself.

Unit 7

Wind

WIND SPEED

The speed of wind depends upon differences in air pressure. Wind speed is measured by an anemometer, a device with cups to catch wind and a gauge to record how fast the cups are turning. The force of wind is measured on the Beaufort Wind Scale that describes the effect of wind on the objects it encounters on the ground. It was developed in 1805 during the era of large sailing ships. The scale goes from 0 to 12.

Beaufort Wind Scale

Force 0—Calm Wind speed less than 1 mile an hour	Chimney smoke rises straight up into the air
Force 1—Light Air Wind speed 2 miles an hour	Smoke drifts very gently
Force 2—Light Breeze Wind speed 6 miles an hour	Leaves rustle and grass moves
Force 3—Gentle Breeze Wind speed 10 miles an hour	Flags flutter in breeze
Force 4—Moderate Wind Wind speed 15 miles an hour	Small branches move
Force 5—Fresh Wind Wind speed 22 miles an hour	Small, thin trees sway
Force 6—Strong Wind Wind speed 28 miles an hour	Large branches move; umbrellas hard to control
Force 7—Near Gale Wind speed 35 miles an hour	Large trees sway
Force 8—Gale Wind speed 43 miles an hour	Twigs break off trees
Force 9—Severe Gale Wind speed 52 miles an hour	Branches break; heavy shingles blow off roofs
Force 10—Storm Wind speed 59 miles an hour	Trees blow down; some damage to houses
Force 11—Severe Storm Wind speed 69 miles an hour	Severe damage to buildings
Force 12—Hurricane Wind speed 73 miles an hour or more	Extreme damage to buildings and widespread damage

Wind

WIND POWER

Man learned to harness the wind thousands of years ago. As early as 4000 B.C., ancient sailors fixed sails to catch the wind and move their boats. Windmills were used for irrigation by the Babylonians by 1700 B.C. Windmills have been used in flat countries, like the Netherlands, for many years to pump water and to grind grain into flour. Wind generators are used in many countries, including the United States, to generate electricity efficiently and inexpensively. Some states, such as California, have large **"wind farms"** of these electricity-creating turbines.

Facts to Remember

- *Wind is the movement of air.*

- *Air moves from areas of high pressure to areas of low pressure.*

- *The Coriolis Effect is the deflection of wind caused by the rotation of the Earth on its axis.*

- *The Beaufort Wind Scale expresses the force of wind in terms of a scale from 0 to 12—from no wind to hurricane-force winds.*

- *Some areas on Earth have constant, prevailing winds.*

- *Local winds can be created by the movement of warm and cool air from land to sea.*

VOCABULARY

atmospheric pressure—*air pressure created by temperature*

Coriolis Effect—*the deflection of winds due to the rotation of Earth*

equator—*an imaginary line around the center of Earth*

high—*high air pressure created by sinking, cold air*

jet stream—*a stream of winds several hundred miles wide*

low—*low air pressure created by rising warm air*

precipitation—*rain or snow*

prevailing wind—*a wind that blows all the time in the same area of Earth*

wind farm—*many wind-driven turbines used to generate electricity*

Wind Vanes

Materials
- *paper or plastic cup*
- *pushpin*
- *modeling clay*
- *new pencil with eraser*
- *straw*
- *tagboard, cardboard, or manila folder*
- *masking tape*
- *scissors*
- *straight pin*
- *magnetic compass*
- *ruler*

Directions

Use with page 65.

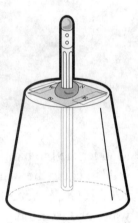

1. Use the pushpin to make a small hole in the middle of the bottom of the paper or plastic cup. Wiggle the pushpin to make the hole larger. Use the point of a pencil to enlarge the hole so that a new unsharpened pencil will fit tightly in the hole.
2. Measure and cut a square piece of tagboard, cardboard, or manila folder that fits the bottom of the cup.
3. Label the square's sides—N, S, E, and W—as shown on the illustration.
4. Place a one-ounce ball of modeling clay in the center of the square.
5. Push the pencil through the hole into the clay so that the pencil stands straight up with the eraser on top.
6. Tape the card firmly to the cup.

Making the Vane

1. Cut out the two triangles on this page.
2. Use the cutouts as a pattern. Draw an outline of each triangle on the tagboard or manila folder.
3. Use the scissors to make a one inch slit in each end of the straw. The slits must line up along the straw.
4. Push the small triangle into the slit at one end of the straw. The triangle point must face <u>away</u> from the straw.
5. Push the large triangle into the other slit. The point of this triangle must face <u>into</u> the slit.

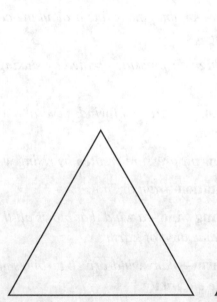
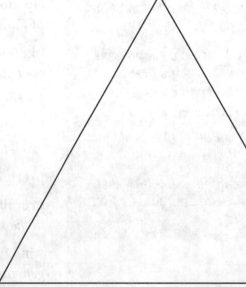

Wind Vanes

Attaching the Vane

Use with page 64.

1. Tape each triangle in place.
2. Use your finger as a balance under the straw.
3. Find the point where the vane balances. It will be a little closer to the large triangle.
4. Use a pushpin to make a hole in the straw at this point so that the triangles are vertical (straight up and down).
5. Use the pushpin or a straight pin to attach the straw to the pencil eraser.
6. Swing the vane several times to make sure that it swings freely and smoothly.

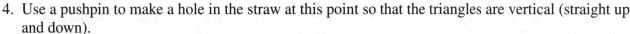

Using the Wind Vane

1. Take the model outside.
2. Use a magnetic compass to locate north.
3. Place the wind vane on a table or on the walkway or playground where there are no barriers to the wind.
4. Face the cardboard base towards the north and tape the cardboard to the cement or asphalt or wood.
5. Watch the small arrow or pointer line up with the wind. The small triangle will point into the wind. This tells you which direction the wind is coming from.

Wind Watching

Record the direction the wind is coming from several times a day.

Date	Time	Direction

Which direction does the wind usually come from at your school during the day? _____

Using the Beaufort Scale

Directions

This activity would be best done on a week with some projected windy weather.

1. Study the Beaufort Wind Scale on page 62.
2. Use this page to record the Beaufort Force of the wind at your school twice a day (in the morning and afternoon) for three days.
3. Base your judgment on your observations of the effect of the wind on flags, trees, blowing papers and leaves, and the other indicators on the chart. Use your pinwheels, windmills, and anemometers to help you choose the appropriate Beaufort Force.

Day 1—Morning

Time: _____

Observations: _____

_____

Beaufort Force Level: _____

Day 1—Afternoon

Time: _____

Observations: _____

_____

Beaufort Force Level: _____

Day 2—Morning

Time: _____

Observations: _____

_____

Beaufort Force Level: _____

Day 2—Afternoon

Time: _____

Observations: _____

_____

Beaufort Force Level: _____

Day 3—Morning

Time: _____

Observations: _____

_____

Beaufort Force Level: _____

Day 3—Afternoon

Time: _____

Observations: _____

_____

Beaufort Force Level: _____

Clouds

DID YOU KNOW THAT . . . ?

- *As many as 500 million tons of water are evaporated and returned to the earth every year.*

- *Jet aircraft create long tube-like clouds called contrails when they release water from their engines.*

- *Lightning forms when electric energy is released from a cloud.*

HOW CLOUDS ARE FORMED

A cloud is a huge mass composed of tiny drops of water floating in the air. Cloud formation begins when **water vapor** is evaporated from the earth through the heat of the Sun. Water vapor may be evaporated from the oceans, other bodies of water, or the ground. The air is warmed by the Sun, and this warm air rises carrying water vapor, an invisible gas. Warm air can hold more water vapor than cool air. As the water vapor rises, the air cools and the water vapor **condenses** into tiny droplets which form a cloud.

The drops of water vapor usually attach themselves to tiny particles of dust, salt, or smoke in the air. Clouds continue forming as long as warm, wet air continues to rise. The highest clouds usually are composed of tiny frozen ice crystals. Lower clouds are composed of water droplets. Eventually, the water held in clouds falls back to the ground as rain or snow.

TYPES OF CLOUDS

Cloud shapes are influenced by wind and the shape of the earth beneath them. There are 10 specific classifications of clouds formed from three major types of clouds. High, wispy, thin clouds are called **cirrus** (meaning feathery) clouds. Low, layered clouds are called **stratus** (meaning layered) clouds. Clouds with huge piles or masses that look like cotton balls are **cumulus** (meaning heaped) clouds. All other shapes of clouds are a mixture or variation of one of these three cloud types. Clouds that are dark brown, gray, or black have the word *nimbus* attached to them. This indicates that these are rain clouds and that rain is likely to fall very soon.

Clouds

CLOUD CLASSIFICATION

Cumulus Clouds

Cumulus clouds are puffy, white masses of clouds with a white or gray base. They look like piles of mashed potatoes, cotton balls, or cauliflower. They are created by thermals that are rising bubbles or currents of warm air. Cumulus clouds can extend from near ground level to over a mile high.

Stratus Clouds

Stratus clouds form in layers that build up and sometimes cover much of the sky. Stratus clouds often bring a persistent drizzle or rain. Stratus clouds are the lowest clouds and often hide hills. They form from ground level to a little over a mile high. They can be even lower and create fog on the ground.

Cirrus Clouds

Cirrus clouds are formed three to eight miles high in the sky. The water vapor in them is frozen into crystals. They may form a complete cloud cover or feathery fragments of high clouds.

Cirrocumulus Clouds

Cirrocumulus clouds look like waves of high white clouds. They often create a regular pattern that looks like fish scales very high in the sky. These clouds indicate that weather may change. They may be more than three to eight miles above the earth.

Cirrostratus Clouds

Cirrostratus clouds are thin, wispy transparent clouds that look like a white veil three to eight miles up in the sky. They often indicate that wet weather is approaching.

Stratocumulus Clouds

The most common clouds are probably stratocumulus clouds. They look like long, low layers of white or gray clouds. They can resemble piles of mashed potatoes split by streaks of sunlight. These clouds may be a mile or more above ground.

Cumulonimbus Clouds

Cumulonimbus clouds are gigantic, flat-topped piles of storm clouds rising from one mile above the ground to several miles into the air. They dominate the sky and often look like they have an anvil on top.

Altostratus Clouds

Altostratus clouds create a thin, white veil across the sky. Some rays of sunlight come through these skimpy clouds that are one to four miles in the air. They can form a colored ring around the Sun and the Moon.

Altocumulus Clouds

Altocumulus clouds are flat lumps of white and gray clouds that look like ravioli. They are mixtures of very cold water and ice. They can indicate thunderstorms in the summer. They are one to four miles above ground.

Clouds

CLOUD CLASSIFICATION *(cont.)*

Nimbostratus Clouds

Nimbostratus clouds are very low-lying clouds less than half a mile above ground. They are black, gray, or dark brown and usually cover the sky entirely blocking out all sunlight. They always indicate snow or rain.

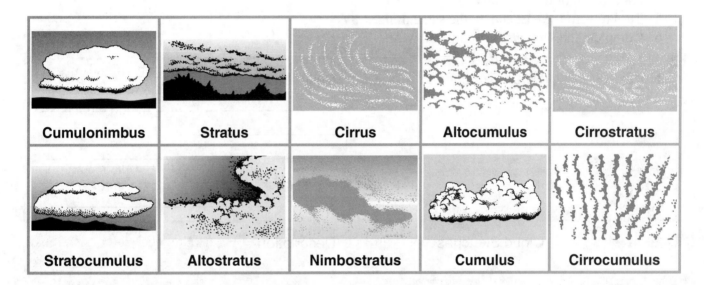

| Cumulonimbus | Stratus | Cirrus | Altocumulus | Cirrostratus |
| Stratocumulus | Altostratus | Nimbostratus | Cumulus | Cirrocumulus |

Facts to Remember

- There are three basic types of clouds and 10 classifications of clouds based on these three types.
- Clouds are classified according to their shape and height.
- Nimbus clouds are dark and usually indicate rain.
- Fluffy, white clouds often form on hot, sunny days and do not indicate rain.
- Clouds are composed of water vapor.
- Warm air holds more water vapor than cold air.
- Water vapor condenses to form clouds in the air.

VOCABULARY

cirrus—*feathery shaped*
condense—*the cooling of water vapor into drops of water*
cumulus—*puffy, heaped, rounded*
stratus—*layered*
water vapor—*water in its gaseous form*

Cloud Study

Directions

This activity needs to be done on a day with clouds of varying types.

1. Take this page outside with a clipboard or pad to write on.
2. Sit on the playground or blacktop facing north.
3. Sketch all of the clouds visible in the north.
4. Use as many descriptive words as possible to describe the height, shape, color, texture, and appearance of these clouds.
5. Turn toward the east and do the same thing.
6. Complete the sections for south and west.

North	Cloud Sketches	Description
		_____
		_____
		_____
		_____
		_____

East	Cloud Sketches	Description
		_____
		_____
		_____
		_____
		_____

West	Cloud Sketches	Description
		_____
		_____
		_____
		_____
		_____

South	Cloud Sketches	Description
		_____
		_____
		_____
		_____
		_____

Student Inquiry Activity

Use the Student Inquiry Worksheets to design and plan your inquiry investigation.

What You Already Know about Clouds

List four facts you have learned about clouds from the readings and activities in this unit.

1. _____
2. _____
3. _____
4. _____

Inquiry Questions

- Can the clouds in your region be used to predict when rain will fall?
- What are the most common clouds in your region in a particular month?
- Do the clouds in your region stay in one location, or are they always moving?

Thinking About Clouds

What would you like to learn about the clouds in your area? List three questions you would like to investigate about clouds.

Inquiry Question #1: _____

_____

Inquiry Question #2: _____

_____

Inquiry Question #3: _____

_____

Making Decisions

Study your question and the questions listed above.

- Which question interests you most?
- Which question is too difficult to do?
- Which question have you chosen?

Your Inquiry Question About Clouds: _____

_____

Planning Your Inquiry

What actions will you need to take to make your inquiry investigation effective, interesting, and scientifically valid? Make a list of your planning steps.

Planning Steps

1. _____
2. _____
3. _____
4. _____

What will you learn from this investigation? _____

_____

Unit
9

Precipitation

PRECIPITATION

All water that forms a cloud and falls to the ground is called **precipitation**. This includes rain, **snow**, **sleet**, drizzle, frost, mist, dew, and **hail**. The temperature of the air determines the type of precipitation that falls.

LIFE GIVING RAIN

Rain is essential to life on Earth. Rain brings water vapor from the clouds to fill the oceans, rivers, lakes, and other bodies of water. It is an essential ingredient in the growth of plants from seeds to mature plants that are used as food by animals and man. A season of **drought** (a period of no rain) can create **famines** (periods of starvation) that kill thousands of people and animals. Too much rain can also create serious problems. Floods destroy crops, damage property, kill people and animals, and also create famines.

RAIN FORMATION

Rain is created in clouds where water vapor has been evaporated from the seas and the land.

Clouds are filled with uncountable trillions of tiny specks of water vapor that are attached to tiny pieces of dust, sand, salt, pollen, smoke, and other bits of debris in the air. Millions of these microscopic droplets of water vapor collide with each other making a single raindrop. This combination of drops is called **coalescence**.

Raindrops are not round. They are shaped like a hamburger bun because they are pushing against air on the way down to the ground. They sometimes look like teardrops when they hit a window, and the surface of the glass slows and shapes their fall.

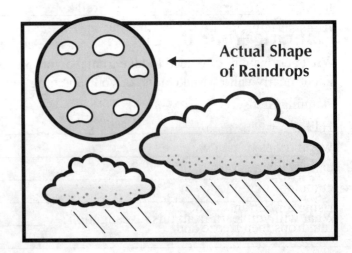

Actual Shape of Raindrops

Precipitation

COLD RAIN

The temperature is below freezing in the clouds above the ground except in the tropical lands near the equator. Ice crystals  form from the millions of specks of water vapor. The crystals collide and grow larger creating snowflakes. If the ground temperature and the air near the ground are relatively warm, the snow crystals melt and become rain as they fall toward the ground. Except in the tropical areas near the equator, most rain starts out as snow and melts to rain as it approaches the ground.

SNOW

Ice crystals form in clouds where the temperature is not just cold but below zero. The temperature may get as cold as 40 degrees below zero. These frozen  ice crystals collide with other crystals as they fall through the air. They will become wet enough to stick together and then freeze into snowflakes as they fall from the cloud toward the ground. Snowflakes will melt into raindrops if the temperature is warm. They may also fall as sleet. If the air temperature is freezing, the snowflakes will land on the ground as snow.

HAIL

Hail is formed when warm drops of rain are carried up into very high cumulonimbus clouds by rising air currents. The  raindrops then freeze and

fall down until another current of rising air lifts them up. The small, frozen balls of hail get another coating of ice. This may happen several times creating larger and larger hailstones. These hailstones can crash into each other in the clouds creating flashes of lightning.

Facts to Remember

- *Rain is essential to life for plants and animals.*

- *Rain is formed in clouds.*

- *Raindrops are formed from millions of specks of water vapor.*

- *Raindrops are not round or teardrop shaped. They are flattened like a hamburger bun.*

- *Most rain starts out as snow which melts before it hits the ground.*

- *Frozen ice crystals collide and form larger crystals that are stuck together as they fall to form snowflakes.*

VOCABULARY

coalescence—*the combination of drops*

drought—*a period of no rain*

famine—*a period of starvation*

hail—*frozen raindrops formed with layers of ice*

precipitation—*water in the air released as a solid or liquid*

sleet—*mixtures of snowflakes and light rain*

snow—*crystals of ice which have collided and formed snowflakes*

Rain Gauge

Materials
- *water bottle*
- *thin marker*
- *scissors*
- *aquarium gravel, sand, or modeling clay*

- *ruler*
- *clear packing tape*
- *masking tape*

Directions

This project would be best done before a heavy rain. It could be done by individuals or teams of two students. The teacher may want to use scissors or a knife to do step one below.

1. Use scissors to cut a slit in a clear water bottle about one inch below the neck of the bottle.

2. Use scissors to cut around the bottle and remove the top.

3. Use masking tape to cover the sharp edges of plastic around the two cut edges.

4. Measure one inch up from the bottom of the base of the bottle and place a line there with a marker.

5. Cover the bottom of the bottle with modeling clay, aquarium gravel, or hard-packed sand to the 1-inch mark exactly.

6. Cut out the 12-centimeter scale shown here. Cover it with clear packing tape to make it waterproof. Use the clear tape to tape it to the bottle with the 0 mark exactly at the 1-inch mark where the clay, sand or gravel ends.

7. Put the top of the bottle upside down like a funnel in the top of the bottle.

8. Set the bottle out in a clear area when rain is about to start.

9. Record the amount of rain in centimeters for each day.

   Day 1 _____

   Day 2 _____

   Day 3 _____

   Day 4 _____

Centimeter Scale

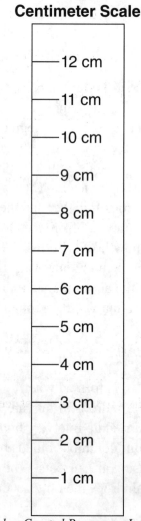

12 cm

11 cm

10 cm

9 cm

8 cm

7 cm

6 cm

5 cm

4 cm

3 cm

2 cm

1 cm

Snow Gauge

Materials
- *various plastic or metal containers—round or square (several inches to one foot deep)*
- *ruler*   • *clear packing tape*

Directions

This activity would be best done by teams of two students on a day when heavy snow is forecast. Students in areas without snow might connect with a classroom by e-mail or pen pals in a part of the country where snow is common in the winter.

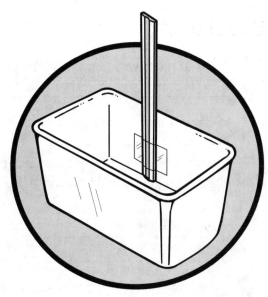

1. Each team should place a waterproof container in an area where snow will fall unhindered.

2. Tape a ruler with inch markings inside the container with clear packing tape.

3. After the snowfall has ended, bring in the container of snow. Measure the height of the snow in the container.

   Height of Snow: _____ inches

4. Allow the snow to melt in the container until only water is left. Measure the height of the water.

   Height of Water: _____ inches

Try This

1. Fill your container of water with snow. Pack it as full of snow as you can and press it until the container is full or the snow is one foot high. Measure the height of the snow in the container.

   Height of Snow: _____ inches

2. Allow the snow to melt in the container until only water is left. Measure the height of the water.

   Height of Water: _____ inches

3. Fill your container with chunks of ice and frozen snow. Pack it as full as possible. Measure the height of the ice in the container.

   Height of Ice: _____ inches

4. Allow the ice to melt in the container until only water is left. Measure the height of the water.

   Height of Water: _____ inches

Drawing Conclusions

How many inches of snow equal one inch of rain? _____

How many inches of ice and frozen snow equal one inch of rain? _____

Student Inquiry Activity

Choosing a Place to Live

What weather conditions do you like best? Do you like dry heat, humid weather, rain, snow, blizzards, cool weather, wind, or thunderstorms?

Make a list of all the weather conditions you enjoy.

1. _____   4. _____
2. _____   5. _____
3. _____   6. _____

Make a list of those weather conditions you really dislike.

1. _____   4. _____
2. _____   5. _____
3. _____   6. _____

Where in the world would you really like to live—if the weather conditions were those you like? Make a list of cities in the United States or throughout the world that might interest you.

1. _____   9. _____
2. _____   10. _____
3. _____   11. _____
4. _____   12. _____
5. _____   13. _____
6. _____   14. _____
7. _____   15. _____
8. _____   16. _____

Doing the Research

Collect almanacs and other books that have detailed weather information. Research the general weather conditions of each of the cities you listed and others that you think of. Use the weather topics listed below and other topics that interest you.

Average daily temperature: _____   Number of days over 90°: _____

Today's high temperature: _____   Number of days below freezing: _____

Yearly snowfall: _____   Number of severe storms: _____

Yearly rainfall: _____   Number of hurricanes: _____

Number of snow days: _____   Number of tornadoes: _____

Number of rainy days: _____   Number of sunny days: _____

Organizing Your Inquiry

1. Use the suggestions listed above to help you organize your search for the best city to live in—as it relates to weather.

2. Collect your resources or Internet sites.

3. Follow the guidelines on the Student Inquiry Worksheets.

Archimedes and Mendeleev

Archimedes

Archimedes was one of the most important scientists of the ancient world. This Greek thinker was the son of a famous astronomer and a student of mathematics, as well as all forms of ancient learning. He was one of the first scientists to use experimentation to test his ideas.

Archimedes achieved fame early and was a personal friend of the king of Sicily who asked him to determine if a gold crown he had ordered was completely gold or had cheaper metals in it. Archimedes was in his bath when he realized that every metal displaced a different amount of water based on its weight and that water could be used to compare the specific weights of irregular objects. Archimedes was reportedly so jubilant at his discovery that he forgot his clothes and ran to the king's palace shouting "Eureka!" ("I've found it!")

Archimedes also studied other aspects of buoyancy and floatation and developed the Archimedes screw which could move water uphill for irrigation. He worked with simple machines and especially explored the mathematical principles of the lever. He said, "Give me a place to stand, and I will move the Earth." He developed an understanding of spirals and computed the value of pi, an essential math concept. Archimedes helped his king create war machines to fight off their Roman enemies. He was accidentally killed by a Roman soldier during a siege of his city.

Mendeleev

Dimitri Mendeleev was born in Russian Siberia in 1834, the youngest of 17 children. His mother worked hard so that he could get a good education in mathematics and science despite his frail health. Dimitri became a high school teacher and later studied physics and math in France and Germany with established scientists. He eventually became a professor at the University of St. Petersburg in Russia.

In 1869 Mendeleev began working on his idea of a single unifying system, a periodic table of the elements in chemistry that had been discovered and those that would be discovered in the future. He arranged the known elements in order by their atomic weights. He also arranged the elements in seven groups according to the physical nature of each element and its chemical properties. Even though only 63 of the 92 natural elements were known at the time, Mendeleev's system left holes to be filled in by future discoveries. He used his table to predict the existence of several elements that were later discovered. One of the man-made elements, number 101, is called *Mendelevium* in his honor. When he died at the age of 73, 86 elements were known and recorded on his table that was used by scientists everywhere.

The Language of Chemistry

DID YOU KNOW THAT . . . ?

- *Neutrons and protons are made of even smaller particles called quarks. These quarks are held together by gluons.*

- *A single tiny speck of dust can have 1,000,000,000,000,000 (one quadrillion) atoms.*

- *Nitrogen is the most abundant element in Earth's atmosphere. About 78% of the atmosphere is nitrogen.*

- *The most common elements in the universe are hydrogen and helium. Together they make up 98% of all the matter in stars.*

- *It would take 17,000,000,000,000,000,000,000,000 (17 septillion) atoms of hydrogen to weigh an ounce (the weight of five pages like this one).*

CHEMICAL LANGUAGE

The language of **chemistry** has many terms. Some of the most important ideas necessary for a basic understanding of chemistry are described on these pages. **Atoms** and **molecules** are the building blocks of **matter**. Matter can be found in three states: solid, liquid, and gas. **Elements**, **compounds**, and **mixtures** express how these atoms and compounds combine to form a huge variety of substances.

STATES OF MATTER

Matter refers to all of the material in the universe. Matter is made up of atoms. There are three normal states of matter: solids, liquids, and gases. Most matter exists in all three states of matter depending on the temperature. At lower temperatures, these forms of matter are solids. Solids can be heated to form liquids. Liquids can be heated to a greater temperature to form gases or vapors. There is a fourth state of matter which occurs when atoms are heated to such a high temperature that electrons separate from

the **nucleus** of their atoms. This state of matter occurring in the Sun and other stars is called *plasma*.

ATOMS

Matter has mass and occupies space. All matter is formed by atoms. These atoms are so small that a million of them would fit in the period at the end of this sentence. As tiny as atoms are, each atom contains three smaller particles: **electrons, protons**, and **neutrons**. Each atom contains a nucleus or center that holds protons and neutrons. Electrons orbit around the nucleus of an atom billions of times in a fraction of a second. Two of these particles have electrical charges. A proton has a positive electrical charge. An electron has a negative charge. A neutron has no charge at all. Usually, each atom has the same number of protons and electrons so that it is neither positively nor negatively charged.

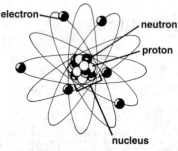

The Language of Chemistry

ELEMENTS

Each element has a different atomic arrangement. All of the atoms in an element are alike. Each element has only one kind of atom. An atom of aluminum always has the same number (13) of protons. An atom of oxygen always has eight protons. Elements may be solids, liquids or gases. There are 92 natural elements in the universe and 24 elements that have been created by scientists in laboratories.

PERIODIC TABLE

The chemical elements are arranged on a periodic table that gives their name, chemical symbol, and atomic number. Elements are arranged in order by their atomic number in 18 columns (groups) and nine rows. Elements that behave in a similar way are close to each other in groups on the table. Elements are placed in rows according to the arrangement of electrons around the nucleus of the atom. This outline of the periodic table gives the atomic number, the chemical symbol, and the name of the chemical elements.

Periodic Table

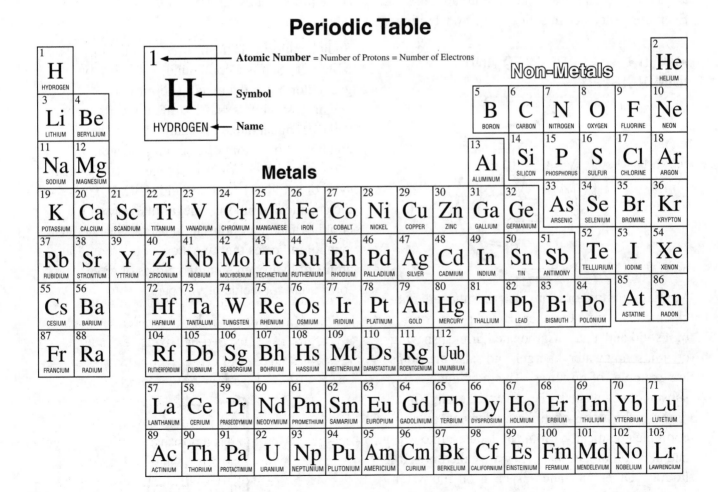

The Language of Chemistry

MOLECULES

A molecule is the smallest part of a chemical element or a compound that can exist on its own. A molecule is formed when two or more elements are held together by a chemical action that is called *bonding*. The electrons in the atoms create the molecular bond by their actions. For example, a single molecule of water has the chemical name H_2O because it is made up of two atoms of hydrogen and one atom of oxygen. Molecules are extremely small. A single drop of water contains 1.7 septillion molecules of water (1,700,000,000,000,000,000,000,000). Molecules of gas in the air and liquids, such as water, are in rapid motion. Even the molecules in solids move by vibrating.

MIXTURES: MISCIBLES AND IMMISCIBLES

Mixtures are two or more materials that are not chemically bound together. Bread is a mixture of a solid and a gas. Carbonated drinks, shaving cream, soapy water, hair gel, and salad dressings are examples of mixtures. The individual substances can usually be separated easily. In a mixture, the atoms of different elements do not combine chemically. Some molecules, like water and alcohol, mix easily. They are called **miscible** liquids. Other substances, such as oil and water are **immiscibles**, materials that do not easily mix.

COMPOUNDS

Unlike a mixture, a compound is a chemical combination of two or more elements held together in molecules that are exactly alike. The chemical bonds that hold molecules of a compound together are not easily broken. Chemists use formulas to identify the make up of each molecule. The formula specifies how many atoms of each element are combined to make the compound. Water is the chemical bonding of two atoms of hydrogen and one atom of oxygen in each molecule of water. The formula for water is H_2O. There are millions of compounds, some produced by nature and others in scientific laboratories.

Sodium chloride is the chemical name for table salt. Salt is a compound of a poisonous gas (chlorine) and a metal (sodium). Its chemical symbol is NaCl. Calcium carbonate is the chemical name for chalk. It is a chemical combining one atom of calcium, one atom of carbon, and three atoms of oxygen. Its chemical symbol is $CaCO_3$. Acetic Acid ($C_2H_4O_2$) is the chemical name for vinegar that is used for cooking and other household uses. The chemical symbol indicates that two atoms of carbon, four atoms of hydrogen, and two atoms of oxygen form every molecule of vinegar.

The Language of Chemistry

DIFFUSION

Diffusion is the process by which molecules of one substance mix with molecules of another substance. Diffusion of molecules occurs when two substances are shaken or stirred. These actions quickly mix the chemicals. Molecules in water collide with other water molecules that are constantly in motion. The addition of chemicals often increases the speed of diffusion as well. Small currents in the water aid the process of diffusion. Heat speeds up the process of diffusion because the molecules move faster in a warm environment than in a cold or frozen one.

Molecules can spread even more rapidly through a gas environment, such as the air in a classroom. Tiny gas molecules of a scent spread easily through the air and are so small that they can go through the pores (invisible, tiny holes) in a balloon or in skin. The smell of food cooking is carried by gas molecules whirling through the air. The scents of perfumes and lotions are carried by molecules that become airborne when sprayed.

Facts to Remember

- *Matter is found in three states: solid, liquid, and gas.*
- *Matter has mass and occupies space.*
- *All matter is made up of atoms.*
- *Atoms contain protons, neutrons, and electrons.*
- *Every element has a unique atomic structure.*
- *The periodic table lists all the natural elements in the universe.*
- *A molecule is the smallest part of a compound which can exist on its own.*
- *Mixtures are not chemically bound together.*
- *Compounds are chemically bound together.*
- *Diffusion is the process by which molecules mix with each other.*

VOCABULARY

atom—*tiny particles of matter*

chemistry—*the study of elements and compounds*

compound—*atoms of different elements bound together*

diffusion—*the process of mixing molecules in a liquid or gas*

electron—*negatively-charged particles orbiting the nucleus of an atom*

element—*a material composed of only one type of atom*

immiscible—*not able to mix easily*

matter—*a substance which has mass and takes up space*

miscible—*able to mix easily*

mixture—*combinations of substances not bound chemically*

molecule—*smallest part of a compound able to exist on its own*

neutron—*particles with no charge in an atom*

nucleus—*the center of an atom with protons and neutrons*

proton—*positively-charged particles in the nucleus of an atom*

The Periodic Table

Directions: Use the Periodic Table on page 79 to help answer the questions on this page. Find the symbol and atomic number for these elements on the Periodic Table.

Element	Symbol	Atomic Number
Uranium	_____	_____
Aluminum	_____	_____
Nitrogen	_____	_____
Calcium	_____	_____
Oxygen	_____	_____
Lead	_____	_____
Iodine	_____	_____
Helium	_____	_____
Sodium	_____	_____
Silicon	_____	_____
Gold	_____	_____
Mercury	_____	_____
Carbon	_____	_____
Iron	_____	_____
Copper	_____	_____
Phosphorus	_____	_____
Boron	_____	_____

Symbols

Directions: Find the names on the Periodic Table to match the symbols listed below.

S _____   Mg _____   K _____

Au _____   Cl _____   O _____

Hg _____   I _____   He _____

C _____   U _____   Ra _____

Na _____   Ar _____   Pb _____

Ca _____   Si _____   N _____

Sn _____   P _____   Ne _____

Try This

Which element has six protons in the nucleus? _____

How do you know? _____

Why isn't water listed as an element? _____

_____

Testing Acids and Bases

Two very common types of compounds are *acids* and *bases*. Acids are commonly found in food, such as lemons and vinegar, and in strong cleaning agents, such as sulfuric acid. Bases are found in soaps and in strong cleaners like ammonia. Bases and acids can be used to neutralize each other. Litmus paper is an indicator that shows whether a liquid is an acid or base. It turns red in an acid and blue in a base. It does not change color in a neutral substance like water or where the acids and bases are mixed in equal strength.

Materials

- *blue and red litmus paper*
- *ammonia*
- *tap water*
- *baking soda*
- *other cleaning liquids*

- *small clear plastic cups*
- *lemon juice*
- *vinegar*
- *apple juice*
- *dish soap*

- *paper towel*
- *salt water*
- *dish soap*
- *other juices*
- *ruler*

Directions

This activity may be done in teams of two. (*Note:* Students should not breathe in fumes from ammonia or other chemicals.)

1. Place a small amount of each liquid listed below into the clear plastic cup. About 1/2 to 1 centimeter or 1 teaspoon of fluid is enough.

2. Test each solution with both colors of litmus paper. Do one liquid at a time and clean the cup each time with a paper towel.

3. Record the color of the litmus paper on the chart below.

4. Then circle the bases listed below. Put a box around the acids. (*Remember:* Bases turn litmus paper blue. Acids turn litmus paper red.)

_____ dish soap	_____ vinegar
_____ lemon juice	_____ baking soda in water
_____ ammonia	_____ apple juice
_____ orange juice	_____ other juice
_____ other cleaners	_____ other liquid
_____ other	_____ salt water

Try This

1. Dip the litmus paper into a small, clear cup of water. Try each color of litmus paper. Did either paper turn a color? _____

2. Stir one centimeter or teaspoon of vinegar with one centimeter or teaspoon of dish soap. Test the solution with each color of litmus paper. What color was the litmus paper? _____

3. Stir one centimeter or teaspoon of vinegar with one centimeter or teaspoon of ammonia. Test the solution with each color of litmus paper. What color was the litmus paper? _____

Secret Writing

During the American Revolution, diplomats stationed in Europe sent secret messages to the Continental Congress written with invisible ink made from tea. The letters were held over a candle, and the message became visible.

> **Materials**
> - *lemons or lemon juice*   • *cotton swab*   • *white paper*
> - *tea*   • *clothing iron*

Directions

1. Compose a secret message to a friend. Use several sentences and write it in pencil on a paper.
2. Use a cotton swab to write your secret message. Dip the swab in lemon juice. Print the message on white paper with the swab. Keep the swab wet with juice.
3. Let the message on the paper dry until it is invisible.
4. Bring the paper to the teacher, so he or she can iron the paper.
5. Give your message to a friend.

Why It Works

The oxidation point (burning point) of lemon juice is lower than that of paper. The dried lemon juice burns quicker or more easily than paper.

Try This

Try the same activity using very strong tea. (Use two or three tea bags in hot water to make the tea.) Describe what happened.

_____

_____

_____

Try the same activity using one or more of these fluids:

- grapefruit juice   • coffee   • orange juice
- tomato juice   • vinegar   • other

Describe what happened.

_____

_____

_____

Soapy Math

Combining dish soap, a detergent, with water and cooking oil creates a soap-film mixture that is a very elastic substance. It can be stretched, but it will always take the shape of the smallest surface area—that is why bubbles or spheres are formed.

Materials
- *2 gallons of water*
- *18 to 20 ounces of dish soap*
- *pail, bussing tray, or other container*
- *5 ounces of vegetable oil*
- *thin wire*
- *straws*
- *scissors*

Making the Soap Solution

Use this page with page 86.

1. Pour two gallons of water into a pail, bussing tray, or other container.
2. Add 18 to 20 ounces of dish soap.
3. Add five ounces of vegetable oil or cooking oil.
4. Stir thoroughly.

Making Flat Shapes

1. Cut straws to make each shape shown below.
2. Thread thin electrical wire or craft wire though the straws and twist it closed to form the figure

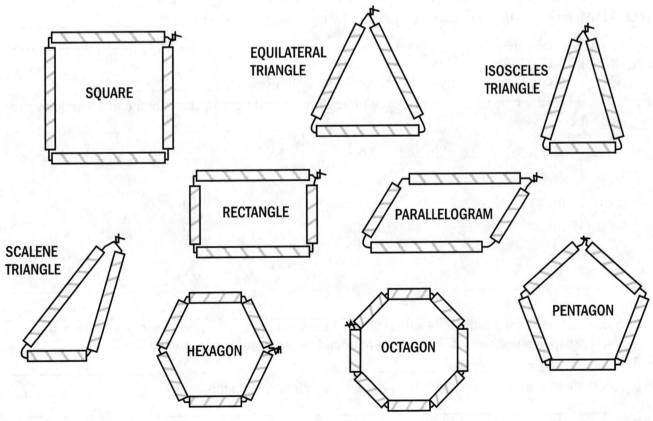

SQUARE

EQUILATERAL TRIANGLE

ISOSCELES TRIANGLE

RECTANGLE

PARALLELOGRAM

SCALENE TRIANGLE

HEXAGON

OCTAGON

PENTAGON

Soapy Math

Making Three-Dimensional Shapes

Use this page with page 85. Use wire and straws to make each of the three-dimensional shapes shown here. You may need to use more than one piece of wire to connect the straws.

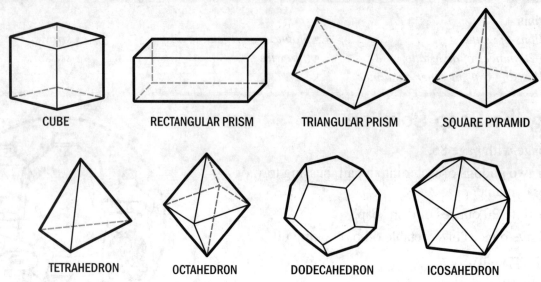

CUBE   RECTANGULAR PRISM   TRIANGULAR PRISM   SQUARE PYRAMID

TETRAHEDRON   OCTAHEDRON   DODECAHEDRON   ICOSAHEDRON

Observations

Dip each of your plane (flat) figures and your three-dimensional figures in the soap film.

1. Can you put a dry finger through the figure without bursting the soapy window? _____
2. Can you put a wet finger through the figure without bursting the soapy window? _____
3. What happens to the film when you pull the figure rapidly through the air? _____
_____
4. Which figure makes the best bubbles? _____
5. Can you see the center of any of the three-dimensional figures? _____
6. Draw a sketch of the inside of two of the three-dimensional figures, showing the lines made by the soap film.

7. What do you see when the light shines through the soap film? (Hold the figure away from your eyes. Soap bubbles burst at 30 miles an hour and the soap might get in your eyes.)
_____
8. What was the most interesting thing you observed about soap bubbles? _____
_____

Student Inquiry Activity

This page will help you get your inquiry activity started. This activity works very well with team of two students.

Reviewing What You Know

Discuss what you have learned about acids and bases with a partner. Then list three things you have learned about acids or bases from the reading and activities in this unit.

1. _____

2. _____

3. _____

Assessing What You Don't Know

Discuss what you don't know about acids and bases with a partner. Then list three things you do not know about acids and bases. Put these in question format.

1. What happens when . . . _____

   _____

2. What happens when . . . _____

   _____

3. What happens when . . . _____

   _____

Suggested Inquiry Questions

- Can you mix an acid and a base so that it is exactly neutral—leaving red litmus paper red and blue litmus paper blue?

- Can you mix an acid and base to make a very mild acid or base with the color of the litmus paper only turning lighter or darker?

- Does salt water dilute or neutralize an acid or a base?

- What is the strongest base you can find in household use?

- Which juice or fruit has the strongest acid?

- How can you test a solid like aspirin to see if it is an acid or base?

- How can you test rain water, pond water, or sea water to determine if they are neutral or slightly acidic?

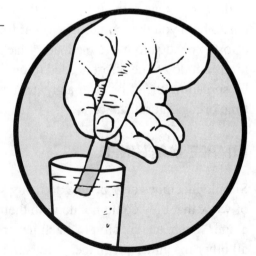

Design an Investigation

Choose one "What happens when . . ." question or Suggested Inquiry Question to investigate. Make sure to get approval from your teacher. Use the Student Inquiry Worksheets to complete your investigation.

Inquiry Question: _____

Unit 11

Simple Machines

DID YOU KNOW THAT . . . ?

● *The Inca Indians of Peru were engineering experts, but they did not have the wheel.*

● *Three rather uncomplicated machines were critical to settling the American West: the steel plow, barbed wire, and portable windmills.*

● *Thomas Jefferson invented a new and more effective design for a wooden plow.*

● *Scientists believe the ski was invented during the Stone Age before the plow or writing.*

MACHINES

Physicists define "**work**" as the total amount of effort needed to move something. A machine is a device that makes this work easier by reducing the amount of **effort** needed to do the work. A **machine** changes the size of the force needed to do work or the direction of the force needed. There are two forces involved in using a machine to do work. One force is the load the machine has to help you overcome. The other force is the effort expended to move the load. Machines of all kinds cut down the effort needed to move a load by spreading the effort over a greater amount of time or a greater distance.

SIMPLE MACHINES

Simple machines help people do many kinds of work that they could not do with their hands alone. There are six simple machines from which all other machines are made. They are the lever, the wheel and axle, the pulley, the inclined plane, the wedge, and the screw.

THE LEVER

The most basic, simple machine and the one which man almost surely used first is the lever. This tool is a bar of wood or metal that sits on a fulcrum or pivoting point. Pushing down on one end of the lever pushes up on the other end of the lever. By carefully choosing where to place the **fulcrum**, the lever can be used to lift heavy objects a short distance or lighter objects a longer distance. Archimedes, the brilliant Greek scientist and inventor, said, "Give me a lever long enough, and I could move the world." The problem, of course, would be what to use as a fulcrum.

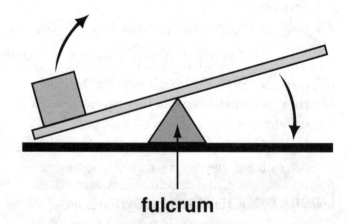

fulcrum

Simple Machines

CLASSES OF LEVERS

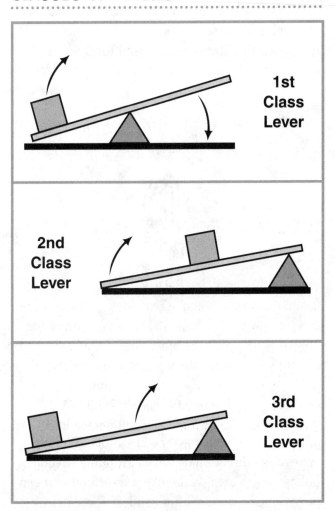

1st Class Lever

2nd Class Lever

3rd Class Lever

There are three classes of levers. Class 1 levers are used to magnify force applied to a job. Class 1 levers include crowbars used to lift heavy objects and pliers used to loosen or tighten nuts. In class 1 levers, the fulcrum is between the **load** and the effort. Class 2 levers also magnify force, but the load is between the fulcrum and the effort. Nutcrackers are class 2 levers. Class 3 levers magnify distance, and the effort is between the load and the fulcrum. Kitchen ice tongs are class 3 levers. The human arm is a class 3 lever. The elbow is the fulcrum.

WHEEL AND AXLE

WHEEL

AXLE

The wheel and axle is sometimes considered the greatest invention in human history, although it certainly has lots of competition for that honor. The wheel makes it possible to move a load over a distance by reducing the friction between the load and the ground. The axle is a shaft within the wheel that allows the wheel to spin freely. When effort is applied to the wheel, the axle magnifies the effort. The axle turns in a much smaller circle, but the force is greater. Cars and bicycles illustrate the application of the wheel and axle.

WEDGE

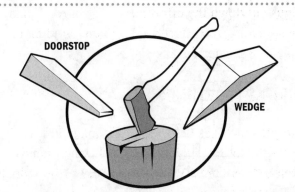

DOORSTOP

WEDGE

The wedge resembles the lever because it is a bar that is thinner on one end than on the other. It is used to separate things. A wooden doorstop presses against the door and keeps it open or closed. An ax is a wedge used to separate fibers in wood. A wedge is a force magnifier. For example, the force of an ax swinging down is magnified in the blade and pushes wood fibers apart.

Unit 11

Simple Machines

INCLINED PLANE

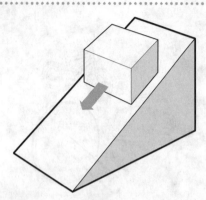

An inclined plane also resembles a lever and is used to lift loads with less effort over short distances. An inclined plane is a force magnifier because it requires less effort to lift the load on an inclined plane than lifting it vertically. A loading ramp at the end of a truck is a good example of an inclined plane. A sidewalk ramp is also an inclined plane.

SCREW

Archimedes screw

A screw is really an inclined plane wrapped around a pole or cylinder. Screws are usually used to fasten things, but they can be used to move some materials. A screw moves into an object with greater force than is used to turn it. One of the great inventions of the ancient world was called the *Archimedes screw*, a device used to lift water from the river to use for irrigation.

The water was lifted a little farther with each turn of the screw. Although the device is named for Archimedes, some versions of this tool were probably invented and used long before Archimedes was born.

PULLEY

A pulley is a variation of the wheel and axle. The wheel of the pulley has a curved center or groove into which a rope or chain fits. Pulleys change the direction of force. Hooking several pulleys in a series works like a lever in that it can move a heavy load with much less force or effort than would be needed without the pulley. The worker will pull a long length of rope to lift a heavy object a short distance. A pulley is hooked between the worker and the force being lifted.

Simple Machines

COMPLEX MACHINES

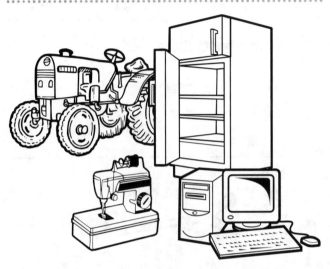

The development of complex versions of machines sparked the Industrial Revolution that literally revolutionized life on Earth. The earliest factory machines were spinning machines and advanced looms that made clothes much cheaper and more available. People moved from the farms to the cities to work in the factories and benefit from cheaper goods. Farms also benefited from industrialization and improved machinery. The invention of the steel plow by John Deere in 1837 sparked a major leap forward in farming. Industrial mechanization continues to this day with constant efforts to increase the speed of manufacture and the quality of the goods. Computer technology in the last 50 years has spurred this process and reorganized transportation, manufacturing, farming, and every aspect of life. But the basic components of these modern machine marvels are still adaptations and combinations of the six basic simple machines.

Facts to Remember

- *Machines make work easier by reducing the effort needed to move a load or change its direction.*

- *There are six simple machines: lever, wheel and axle, wedge, inclined plane, screw, and pulley.*

- *There are three classes of levers depending upon the location of the fulcrum, effort, and load.*

- *The wheel and axle reduces friction as it moves a load over a distance.*

- *A wedge is used to separate things, such as wood fibers.*

- *An inclined plane reduces the effort to lift a load.*

- *A screw is used to fasten things or move things.*

- *A pulley uses a wheel and a rope to lift a load over short distances.*

- *Complex machines are combinations of simple machines.*

VOCABULARY

effort—*the energy used to move a load or change its direction*

fulcrum—*the support for a lever*

load—*the force to be moved*

machine—*a device to change the size or direction of a force*

work—*the effort used to move a load*

Identifying Simple Machines

Directions: Label each tool on the page with at least one of the simple machines that is a basic component of the tool.

Lever	Inclined Plane	Wheel and Axle	Screw	Wedge	Pulley

yo-yo

bicycle handlebars

rake

shovel

human arm

drill bit

egg beater

scissors

knife

teeter-totter

slide

skateboard ramp

92

Finding Simple Machines

Directions: Make a list of all the tools or items you can find that you think are simple machines. Then label the kind of simple machine. One example is done for you. On the back, you can illustrate each tool or machine with a simple sketch. (This activity may be done at home or at school alone or with a partner.)

Tool/Machine   **Kind of Simple Machine**

wheel chair ramp   inclined plane

_____   _____

_____   _____

_____   _____

_____   _____

_____   _____

_____   _____

_____   _____

Try This

Examine a bicycle or an automobile. Make a list of every part that you can also identify as a simple machine. Use a sketch if you do not know the part's name.

Bicycle/Car Part   **Simple Machine**

_____   _____

_____   _____

_____   _____

_____   _____

Toys and Machines

Materials
- *children's toys*
- *toothpicks*
- *masking tape*
- *straws*
- *stiff cardboard*
- *bottle caps*
- *scissors*
- *string or fishline*
- *small wheels*

Simple Machines in Toys

This activity may be done at home or at school alone or with a partner. Use this page with the inquiry activity on page 95.

1. Find a supply of younger children's toys from a younger sibling, a kindergarten room, or a toy display at a store.
2. Study the toys one at a time. Look for all of the examples of simple machines that are evident on each toy.
3. Name the toy and draw a sketch of each toy or part of a toy. Label the simple machines on your sketch.

Toy Name: _____
Labeled Sketch

Toy Name: _____
Labeled Sketch

Toy Name: _____
Labeled Sketch

Toy Name: _____
Labeled Sketch

Your Own Simple Machines

1. Make a small model of each of the six simple machines. Use pieces of toys, straws, toothpicks, string, bottle caps, small wheels, stiff cardboard, and other available materials. Label each machine with masking tape.
2. Combine two of your simple machines to make a tool or toy. It could be two straws used as levers to make scissors or pliers. It could be a bottle cap wheel and axle with string to make a pulley and a cardboard ramp.
3. Draw sketches here to illustrate your simple machine combinations.

Sketch #1

Sketch #2

Sketch #3

Sketch #4

Student Inquiry Activity

Use page 94 as a lead-in to this activity. This activity can be done alone or by a team of two students.

Inventing with Simple Machines

Examine each of the simple machine models you found on page 94. Think about the uses for each of these simple machines as you touch and play with them.

- What experiments could you do with these simple machines?
- What invention could you make using two or more of these simple machines?
- What children's toy could you create with some of these simple machines?
- What game could you make with these simple machines?
- What useful tool could you design for you or your family with these machines?
- What other materials would you need?

Thinking on Paper

Draw three sketches of possible inventions, toys, or experiments you could do with the simple machines and other easy-to-find materials. Be imaginative! Be creative! Let your mind loose!

Sketch #1 Idea: _____

Sketch #2 Idea: _____

Sketch #3 Idea: _____

Selecting Your Simple Machines Inquiry Project

Which of your ideas do you like best? _____

Why do you like it? _____

What help will you need to do the investigation? _____

Get Started

Collect your materials. Follow the guidelines on the Student Inquiry Worksheets.

Unit 12

Motion

LAWS OF MOTION

Isaac Newton

Every form of movement is governed by absolute laws of physics. These laws have been discovered by scientists such as Isaac Newton. As a young man, Isaac Newton formulated the three fundamental laws of motion that are the center of our understanding of motion. Motion comes in many forms. It may be linear and thus move in a straight line. It may oscillate, which means to move back and forth like a pendulum. Circular motion is called **centripetal force**. This motion moves in a circle around a fixed object.

NEWTON'S FIRST LAW OF MOTION

An object will remain at rest (unmoving) or will continue traveling at a constant speed in a straight line unless acted upon by an outside force. This means that an object that is not moving will not begin to move unless it is acted upon by an outside force. A hockey puck sitting on the ice doesn't start moving until it is hit. The second part of the law says that the object in motion will continue at the same speed and in the same direction until it is acted upon by an outside force. For example, a moving hockey puck will not change speed and direction until it is hit.

Motion

THE SECOND LAW OF MOTION

The second law of motion states that the rate at which an unmoving object moves from its position at rest or the extent to which a moving object will be diverted from its straight line path is dependent upon the mass of the object and the force which is applied to it. An unmoving object like a hockey puck sitting on the ice will be affected by the amount of force with which it is hit. It will move much farther than a heavy rock hit by the same force.

A moving object may speed up or slow down depending upon the **force** applied. Friction is a force that causes all moving things on Earth to slow down. A hockey puck will slow and stop due to the friction of the ice. A baseball will fall due to air resistance. The **mass** of an object (the amount of matter in an object) determines how much the object is affected by the outside force. A bowling ball hit by a bat will not be diverted or slowed as much as a baseball will be. The amount or size of the force also affects the object in motion. A huge adult hitting a baseball will change its direction much more than a child will.

THE THIRD LAW OF MOTION

For every action, there is an equal and opposite reaction. If a force pushes in one direction, an equal force pushes in the opposite direction. If a rocket takes off into the sky, the amount of force it exerts going up is equaled by the amount of force exerted against the ground as it takes off. The push of the gases out of the base of the rocket engines pushes the rocket forward. A runner pushes against the starting block when he races forward. There is an equal push from the block as he takes off.

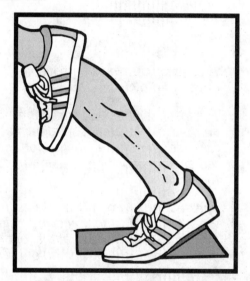

UNIVERSAL LAW OF GRAVITATION

The larger two objects are and the closer they are, the greater will be the gravitational attraction between the objects. The size and weight of the first object, the size and weight of the second object, and the distance between the two objects determine the intensity of the attraction. Earth and Moon are about 250,000 thousand miles apart. If the distance were doubled to 500,000 miles, the gravitational attraction would be only ¼ of the current attraction.

Unit
12

Motion

CENTRIPETAL FORCE

An object moving in a circle is constantly being pulled toward the center of the circle by centripetal force. If you swing a hammer around in a circle, centripetal force will constantly change the direction of the hammer and pull the hammer inward keeping the hammer moving in a circular motion. If you stop, the hammer will fly off in a straight line following Newton's laws of motion. Roller coasters demonstrate centripetal force when they do loops or circles. The force is directed toward the center of the circle and held in place by the walls and tracks.

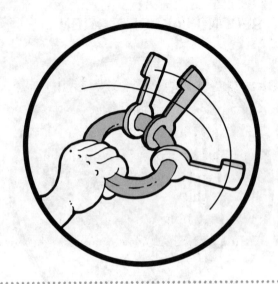

Facts to Remember

- There are three laws of motion developed by Isaac Newton.

- The first law of motion states that an object at rest tends to remain at rest and an object in motion tends to remain in motion unless acted upon by an outside force.

- The second law of motion states that the rate at which an unmoving object moves from its position at rest or the extent to which a moving object will be diverted from its straight line path is dependent upon the mass of the object and the force which is applied to it.

- The third law of motion states that for every action, there is an equal and opposite reaction.

- The Universal Law of gravitation states that all objects are attracted to each other, and the attraction is dependent upon the mass of the objects and their distance from each other.

- Centripetal force is a force created by circular motion that pulls a rotating object toward the center.

SPECIAL TERMS

These terms are often used when describing motion. It is helpful to be familiar with them.

acceleration—*rate of change of velocity*

centripetal—*a force that pulls rotating objects towards the center of rotation*

equilibrium—*a balance between forces*

force—*a push or pull on any object*

gravity—*the attraction of all objects towards each other*

inertia—*the tendency of an object at rest to remain at rest*

mass—*the amount of matter in an object*

momentum—*the mass of an object times its velocity*

velocity—*the rate of speed of an object in one direction*

Centripetal Spinners

Materials
- *small paper clip*
- *straw*
- *large paper clips*
- *scissors*
- *masking tape*
- *fishline*

Making a Centripetal Spinner

1. Cut a piece of fishline about 15 inches long.
2. Cut a straw in half.
3. Tape four large paper clips in a bundle.
4. Tie one end of the fishline to a small paper clip. Make sure the knot is tight.
5. Feed the fishline through the straw.
6. Tie the other end of the fishline to the bundle of large paper clips.

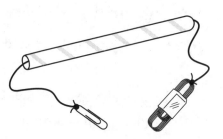

Using the Spinner

1. Set the bundle of large paper clips in the palm of one hand and hold the straw between the fingers of your other hand.
2. Gently rotate or spin the straw in a tight circle.
3. The smaller paper clip at the end of the fishline should spin out in a circle and lift the bundle of large paper clips off your palm.
4. Hook one more large paper clip to the bundle.
5. Rotate the straw.
6. Does it lift the five paper clips? _____
7. Keep hooking large paper clips to the bundle, one at a time.
8. How many large paper clips could you get the spinner to lift with just the one small paper clip at the top?

   _____

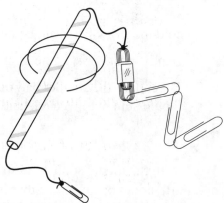

Try This

Use a piece of fishline about 18 to 20 inches long. Make the same model with the longer line.

Was the model easier or harder to control? _____

How many large paper clips could you pick up with this model? _____

Centripetal Spinners

Materials
- *small paper clips*
- *straw*
- *modeling clay*
- *scissors*
- *masking tape*
- *fishline*

Making an Earth-Moon Model

(*Note:* This page should be used after page 99.)

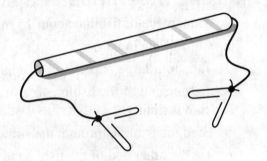

1. Cut a piece of fishline about 15 inches long.

2. Tie a small paper clip tightly to one end of the fishline.

3. Feed the fishline through a straw.

4. Tie another small paper clip to the other end of the fishline.

5. Bend both paper clips open like a mouth.

6. Mold one-half ounce of modeling clay (half of one finger-sized strip of clay) onto the open paper clip on one end of the model. Shape it into a round ball like the moon.

7. Mold one and one-half ounces of modeling clay (one and one-half finger-sized strips of clay) onto the open paper clip on other end of the model. Shape it into a round ball like Earth.

8. Be sure the clay on both ends is wrapped firmly around the open paper clips, so it will not fly off.

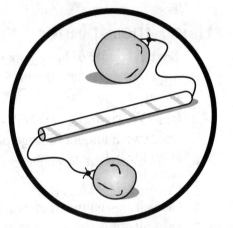

Using the Model

1. Set Earth (the large ball of clay) in the palm of one hand and hold the straw between the fingers of your other hand.

2. Gently rotate or spin the straw in a tight circle.

3. The moon (the smaller ball of clay) at the end of the fishline should spin out in a circle and lift the Earth bundle off your palm.

Try This

Work with the model so that the straw is in the middle and the moon and Earth are in balance. Neither is pulling the other up and down. (A slow or gentle rotation of the straw usually works.) The model illustrates the gravitation pull of Earth and the moon.

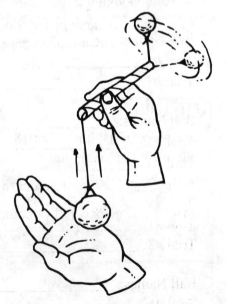

Gravity

Materials
- *balls of many sizes and weights*
- *stepladders, chairs, or stairs*

Directions

This activity works very well in two-person teams.
1. Hold two balls of equal sizes but different weights, such as a tennis ball in one hand and a heavy ball of modeling clay or a baseball in the other.
2. Climb a few rungs of a stepladder, stand on a chair, or climb a staircase.
3. Hold the balls directly in front of you so that they are exactly the same distance from the ground.
4. Count to three and let the balls drop at exactly the same time.
5. One partner should observe which ball lands first or if they land at the same time.
6. Take turns dropping the balls. Do several trials and record the results below.

Tennis ball/Clay ball

Trial #1: _____   Trial #2: _____

Trial #3: _____   Trial #4: _____

Different Sizes/Different Shapes

1. Hold two balls of different sizes, such as a tennis ball in one hand and a basketball in the other.
2. Hold the balls on a stepladder or stairs as you did before. Be sure to drop the balls at exactly the same time.
3. One partner should observe which ball lands first.
4. Do this experiment with balls of many different sizes and shapes.
5. Do four trials for each pair of balls. Record the balls used and the results on this page.

Ball Names: _____

Trial #1: _____   Trial #2: _____

Trial #3: _____   Trial #4: _____

Ball Names: _____

Trial #1: _____   Trial #2: _____

Trial #3: _____   Trial #4: _____

Ball Names: _____

Trial #1: _____   Trial #2: _____

Trial #3: _____   Trial #4: _____

Ball Names: _____

Trial #1: _____   Trial #2: _____

Trial #3: _____   Trial #4: _____

Gas Rocket

This activity illustrates Newton's third law of motion—"For every action, there is an equal and opposite reaction."

Materials
- *clear plastic water bottle*
- *vinegar (any color)*
- *fishline*
- *meter stick or yardstick*
- *baking soda*
- *facial tissue*
- *scissors*
- *index card (optional)*
- *masking tape*
- *tablespoon*
- *corks*
- *chalk*

Directions For Dry Fuel

1. Pour one tablespoon of baking soda into a sheet of flat facial tissue.
2. Spread the baking soda along the length of the tissue.
3. Fold the tissue into a long tube with the baking soda along the entire length of the tube.
4. Cut four three-inch long pieces of fishline.
5. Tie a piece of fishline at each end of the tube and two pieces along the tube.

Making the Rocket

1. Tear off any paper from the clear plastic water bottle. Make sure there are no holes in the bottle.
2. Pour six ounces of vinegar into the bottle.
3. Wrap several layers of masking tape around the cork to seal any holes in the side of the cork.
4. Carefully twist the tape-covered cork into the top of the bottle to make sure it will form a very tight seal.
5. Draw an astronaut on a piece of index card and tape it to the cork if you wish.

Cork should
fit tightly
into bottle

Firing the Rocket

1. Use a meter stick or a yardstick to measure the distance on the blacktop area you will use as a firing range. Use chalk to label every five meters or yards.
2. Bring your baking soda tube and bottle separately to the firing line.
3. When you are ready, take out the cork and drop the long, thin tube of baking soda into the bottle.
4. Quickly twist the cork tightly into the bottle.
5. <u>Do not point the bottle at your face</u>. <u>Point it away</u>. Point the bottle down range and shake it vigorously until the bottle begins to swell.
6. Hold the bottle tightly until the cork flies out. You should feel the reaction in your hands as the bottle pushes back.
7. Measure the distance your cork rocket traveled.

Student Inquiry Activity

Materials
- *fishline*
- *index cards or tag board*
- *straws*
- *balloons*
- *markers*
- *tape*
- *pushpins*
- *scissors*

Directions for Balloon Rocket

This inquiry investigation begins with an activity and leads to your creative modifications. This inquiry activity works well as a team activity. Use the Student Inquiry Worksheets to design and plan your inquiry investigation.

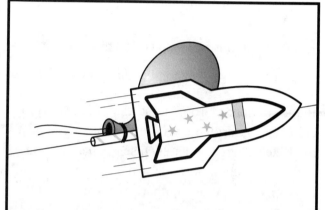

1. Connect a piece of fishline several feet long from one part of your room to another. Use pushpins or tape to secure the line.

2. Use an index card or tag board to design a rocket like the one shown here and cut it out. Use markers to decorate it.

3. Tape a straw to one side of the rocket so that it will travel along the fishline.

4. Blow up a balloon, pinch it to keep the air in it, and slide the straw onto the fishline.

5. Release the balloon and observe how well the rocket travels along the fishline.

Inquiry Investigation: Making Modifications

- What modifications can you create to make the balloon rocket fly faster and farther?
- How would the shape of different balloons affect the rocket's flight?
- What design changes could you make to the rocket to make it fly better? Would it be better if it was longer, wider, or thicker?
- How could the angle of the fishline be improved to create a better flight?
- Would longer or thicker or narrower straws work better?
- Could you connect two balloons effectively?

Planning Your Inquiry

Decide on a list of the modifications you can try to improve your balloon rocket. Follow the guidelines on the Student Inquiry Worksheets.

Isaac Newton

Isaac Newton was born on Christmas day in 1642 and died in 1727. In the course of his long life, he made some of the most important discoveries in modern science and fundamentally changed the way the universe was perceived by scientists. In the minds of many scientific historians, he was the greatest scientist of all time.

A great English poet wrote of him:

"Nature and Nature's laws lay hid in night:

God said, "Let Newton be! and all was light."

In the summer of 1665 at the age of 23, Newton's college, Cambridge University, was closed because the Black Plague, a deadly disease, had hit London and was killing thousands. The next 18 months that Newton spent on his mother's farm produced the greatest discoveries in the history of science in any brief span of time.

Newton discovered the binomial theorem in mathematics, a major development in algebra. He worked out the basic concept of calculus, which he called "fluxions"—a kind of math essential today to space travel, understanding the mathematics of space, and creating complicated calculating devices. We simply could not put a man in space without the calculations made possible by calculus.

In this same period, Newton discovered the Universal Law of Gravitation. This law states that all objects in the universe are attracted to each other and that the force of the attraction depends on how large each body is and how far away they are. Newton's "inverse law of gravitation" means that if the moon were twice as far from Earth as it is, the gravitational pull would only be one-fourth of its present force.

Newton also worked out the three laws of motion described earlier in this unit. These laws and the Universal Law of Gravitation are the very backbone of modern physics. He was also the first scientist to prove that white light is composed of the seven colors of the spectrum. He devised an experiment in which he used one prism to separate the colors and a second one to recombine the colors into white light. Newton also invented the reflecting telescope.

Newton spent the rest of his life refining his ideas and publishing books about his ideas. His *Principia Mathematica* published in 1687 is considered the most important scientific book ever published. He did exhaustive studies of the moon, carried on experiments trying to convert cheap metals into gold, and completely revised the method of running a government mint to coin money. Newton never married and often had trouble keeping friends. He was the first scientist to be honored by burial in Westminster Abbey.

Pendulums, Gyroscopes, and Friction

DID YOU KNOW THAT . . . ?

● *In 1582, Galileo discovered the regularity of a pendulum's swing after observing the swing of a chandelier in a church.*

● *The first pendulum clock was made in 1657 by the Dutch astronomer Christiaan Huygens.*

PENDULUM

A **pendulum** is made by suspending a weight by a piece of string or wire from a single, fixed point. When the weight is hanging motionless directly below the fixed point where it is attached, the pendulum is in a state of **equilibrium** or balance. If the weight is moved to one side of this position of equilibrium and then released, gravity will pull the weight back toward the center and momentum will carry the weight beyond the point of equilibrium to the other side. The same gravitational force slows it down on the other side and pulls it toward the middle point of equilibrium and past again. The weight will swing in this very regular movement until friction created by air eventually causes the pendulum to stop again and remain suspended in a state of equilibrium. This kind of back and forth motion is called **oscillation** or **vibration**.

fixed point

string

plumb bob

swing arc

point of equilibrium

PENDULUM PERIODS AND BOBS

The time it takes a pendulum to make one complete swing forward and back is called the *period*. The size of the swing or movement of the pendulum is called the *amplitude*. The number of times the pendulum vibrates (completes once back and forth swing) in once second is called the **frequency**. The time it takes the pendulum to make one complete swing is affected entirely by the length of the string. This is the distance from the fixed point to the weight. The weight of the pendulum, which is called the **bob**, does not affect the time of the period. Therefore, a light weight on a long string will take longer to swing than a heavy weight on a short string. Pendulums are used in some clocks because the timing is so regular. A mechanism in the clock pushes the pendulum to keep it moving back and forth.

Unit 13

Pendulums, Gyroscopes, and Friction

GYROSCOPES

A **gyroscope** is made by a wheel mounted securely on an axle. The wheel and axle are then usually mounted to a frame. A gyroscope pushes against any force or effort to tilt it while it is spinning. The pivot or bottom point of a spinning gyroscope can be balanced on a very small object. The gyroscope will spin on a point, such as a colored marker cap or a spot on the floor, until the spin is slowed down by friction.

A gyroscope demonstrates the type of motion called **angular momentum**. This spinning motion resists the forces of gravity trying to topple the gyroscope. The inertia created by the spinning wheel provides stability. The force of gravity is constantly pushing against the gyroscope, but the center of the gyroscope called the *axis* (the axle) is in constant motion at right angles to the force of gravity.

A top is a toy gyroscope that demonstrates the way such an instrument works. It will spin on its axis until friction overcomes the toy, and it slows down and falls over. Any gyroscope has a unique effect called **precession**. If you push against the spinning gyroscope, it does not move in the direction of the push. It moves at right angles to the push. Precession is the same movement that keeps a bicycle wheel upright when you are pedaling.

USING GYROSCOPES

In addition to children's toys, gyroscopes are used in instruments to counteract the rolling motion of a ship or plane. These instruments are called *gyrostabilizers*. A navigational gyrocompass keeps planes and ships pointing north or in any desired direction.

FRICTION

Friction is a force that keeps objects from moving easily against each other. Friction occurs because no object is perfectly smooth. Even the smoothest-appearing materials have tiny rough pieces that catch on the surface they are rubbing against. The rougher two surfaces are, the more friction exists when they move against each other.

Pendulums, Gyroscopes, and Friction

USING FRICTION

If friction did not exist, you would not be able to walk because your feet or shoes would slide around like a pool ball on a skating rink. Friction between the rubber on tires and the asphalt on the roads keeps cars from sliding around and into each other. Friction between a nail and the wood it is driven into holds the nail in place. Buildings would fall down without the friction created between many of its building materials. Even molecules of air create friction. You can feel this air resistance when riding a bike or in an open convertible. This friction increases greatly when speed increases. Friction between any two surfaces causes heat.

OVERCOMING FRICTION

Friction has many uses, but it is also a force that man is constantly contending with. Bicycles and automobiles need friction to stay on the road, but too much friction can slow vehicles down and limit their speed and performance. So engineers try to balance these needs. Brakes use friction to stop, but **lubricants** are used to keep wheels freely moving on their axles. Some of the ways used to reduce friction are to make two surfaces smooth so that they slide easily against each other. Oil, water, and other lubricants are used to reduce friction. Ball bearings are small, round, rolling objects that can reduce friction between moving parts of a machine.

Facts to Remember

● *The weight of the bob on a pendulum does not affect the length of the period.*

● *Gyroscopes use angular momentum to remain in motion until friction slows down the gyroscope.*

● *Friction provides many uses to man and offers challenges to be overcome.*

VOCABULARY

angular momentum—*spinning motion like a gyroscope*

bob—*the weight of the pendulum*

equilibrium—*state of balance*

frequency—*number of vibrations per second*

friction—*force that keeps objects from moving easily against each other*

gyroscope—*a wheel and axle mounted in a frame and rotating on a pivot point*

lubricant—*oil or other liquids used to reduce friction*

oscillation —*back and forth movement*

pendulum—*a weight suspended on a string from a fixed point*

precession—*an effect when a push against a spinning gyroscope creates movement at right angles to the push*

vibration—*back and forth movement*

Making Small Gyroscopes

Materials
- *pushpin*
- *barbecue wood skewers*
- *ruler*
- *modeling clay*
- *sharp pencils*
- *math compass*
- *thick toothpick (round or square)*
- *tagboard, manila folder, and/or construction paper*
- *scissors*
- *plastic cups*
- *masking tape*

Directions

Use this page with page 109. These tops can be made with a variety of materials. Use what you have.

1. Use a math compass or a round object, such as the top of a plastic cup, to draw a circle on a piece of tagboard, manila folder, or stiff construction paper.

2. Carefully cut out the round disk you drew.

3. Use a ruler to help you find the exact center if you did not use a compass.

4. Use a pushpin to make the hole. Wiggle the pushpin to make the hole a little larger.

5. Push a round toothpick or a large square toothpick through the center hole. Tape the toothpick in place if it does not fit tightly.

Using the Top

Find a flat area to spin your model.

How long will the model spin before it stops or falls over?

_____

Do several trials. What is the longest time it stayed upright?

_____

Try This

1. Make another model using a different size of paper or tagboard.
2. Use a different kind of toothpick or a small, sharpened pencil as the axle.
3. Spin the model.
4. What is the longest time you could get the top to spin? _____

Making Small Gyroscopes

Improving the Design

Use with page 108.

1. Use a math compass or a cup to make a circle about two inches in diameter on a piece of stiff tagboard or thin cardboard.
2. Use scissors to cut out the disk.
3. Use a ruler or the compass point to find the exact center of the round disk.
4. Use a pushpin to make a hole in the center and wiggle the pushpin to make the hole a little wider.
5. Use a sharpened pencil to push through the hole and make the axle. Be sure the pencil fits very tightly or is taped in place.
6. Use modeling clay to make a tapering, top-like shape below the round disk like the one shown in the illustration.

Testing Your Top

Spin your model. Do several trials. Record your results.

First trial: _____ seconds   Second trial: _____ seconds

Third trial: _____ seconds   Fourth trial: _____ seconds

Fifth trial: _____ seconds   Sixth trial: _____ seconds

Making Other Models

1. Use longer pencils, barbecue skewer sticks, larger tagboard disks, modeling clay, and other materials to make a variety of models.
2. Test each model, sketch it in the space below, and record your results.

Model #1 Sketch	Results
	_____
	_____
	_____
	_____

Model #2 Sketch	Results
	_____
	_____
	_____
	_____

Try This

Use a small cardboard box as a frame and attach your top like a gyroscope.

Working with Pendulums

Materials
- *fishline*
- *watch or clock*
- *masking tape*
- *large paper clips*
- *ruler*
- *tape*
- *washers*
- *wire hangers, dowels, inexpensive bamboo garden stakes, broomsticks, or yard sticks*

Directions

1. Straighten the hanger so it is about two feet long. (You can use wood dowels, inexpensive bamboo garden stakes, or yardsticks instead of a hanger.)

2. Tape the straightened hanger between two desks of the same height, about 18 to 24 inches apart.

3. Cut a piece of fishline about 16 inches long.

4. Tie one end of the fishline securely to the center of the hanger.

5. Use a ruler to measure one foot down from the hanger.

6. Tape four large paper clips or washers together to form the bob of the pendulum.

7. Tie the bob to this end of the line one foot from the hanger.

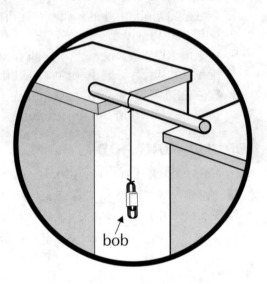

bob

Using the Pendulum

1. Hold the bob extended the length of the fishline and even with the level of the hanger and desks.

2. Release the bob. How long does the pendulum swing before it is completely still?

_____

3. Hold the bob extended the length of the fishline and even with the level of the hanger and desks.

4. Release the bob. How many complete swings does the pendulum make before it is completely still? (A complete swing is one movement back and forth.) _____

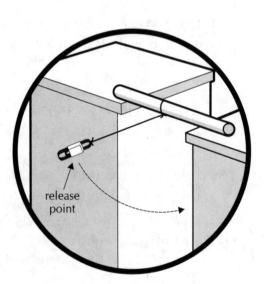

release point

Working with Pendulums

The Weight of the Bob

Use this with page 110.

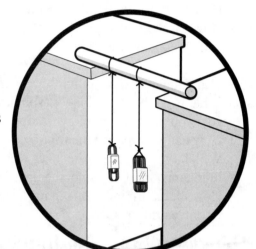

1. Move the desks as far apart as you can and still securely hold the hanger between them.

2. Move the pendulum you have been using to one side of the space between the desks.

3. Tape eight large paper clips together to form a bob twice as heavy as the one you have been using.

4. Cut another piece of fishline about 16 inches long and suspend the bob on this pendulum exactly the same length as the other one. Adjust the fishline until you are certain they are an even length.

5. Adjust the two pendulums on the hanger until they are far enough apart not to swing into each other or to swing into the sides of the desks.

6. Hold the two bobs at their full length, even with the level of the hanger and the desks.

7. Release the bobs at the same time.

8. Observe the speed of the bobs and how they swing. Adjust the bobs if they get tangled and try again.

9. Do at least three trials of the bobs. Describe what happened.

_____

_____

10. Do you think the weight of the bob affects the speed of the swing?

_____

The Length of the Pendulum

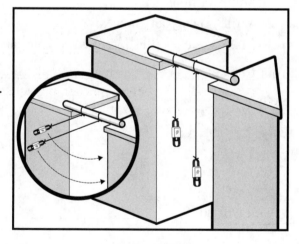

1. Remove the heavier bob. Leave the original pendulum in place.

2. Cut a piece of fishline two feet long.

3. Make a four-paper clip bob just like the original one. Tie one end of the fishline to the bob.

4. Use a ruler to measure exactly 18 inches from the hanger and tie the other end of the fishline so that this pendulum hangs exactly 18 inches from the hanger.

5. Arrange the two pendulums on the hanger so that they will not swing into each other or the sides of the desk.

6. Hold the two bobs at their full length, even with the level of the hanger and the desks.

7. Release the bobs at the same time. Observe the speed of the bobs and how they swing.

8. Describe what happened. _____

Student Inquiry Activity

Inquiry Questions

- How long can you make a pendulum swing?
- How can you illustrate the pattern made by a swinging pendulum using sand, glue, paint, or glitter?
- What happens when you use two pendulums connected to a fishline frame instead of wood or a hanger?
- Can you get two pendulums to swing at the same time with one just as fast as the other?
- What is the best and longest-spinning top you can make?
- Can you make a model gyroscope in a frame?
- How can you reduce the friction between a heavy box and a road?
- Which type of friction-reducer works best to move a brick or cement block along a board—lubricants, marbles, smooth sticks like pencils, or other materials?
- How much tire inflation—hard, medium, soft, or very soft—reduces friction for a bicycle and improves riding speed?

Thinking About the Inquiry Suggestions

1. Read the inquiry suggestions listed above.
2. Cross out the choices that do not interest you or that you cannot do because of lack of materials.
3. Put a box around each choice that seems interesting.

Brainstorming

List three inquiry questions about pendulums, gyroscopes, and/or friction that you would like to test.

1. _____
2. _____
3. _____

Directions

1. Choose one of the suggested inquiry questions or an inquiry idea of your own from the brainstorming list.
2. Write down your choices.
3. Make sketches illustrating what materials and arrangements you might use to test your inquiry.

Your Choice: _____

Sketch

Materials: _____

_____

_____

_____

What I will do: _____

_____

Completing the Inquiry

Do the motion inquiry investigation that you planned. Use your Student Inquiry Worksheets for guidance and to record data.

Electromagnetic Radiation

DID YOU KNOW THAT . . . ?

● *Gamma rays can be produced by stars falling into black holes or collisions between neutron stars.*

● *Ultraviolet radiation on Earth comes from the Sun or very hot objects.*

● *Pulsar stars produce beams of radio waves.*

● *Everybody produces some infrared radiation.*

WAVE ENERGY

There are several types of wave energy that are part of a **spectrum** called **electromagnetic radiation**. These types of wave energy include radio waves, television waves, radar waves, microwaves, infrared waves, visible light, ultraviolet waves, x-rays, and gamma rays. Different parts of the spectrum have different levels of energy. Radio waves at one end of the spectrum are low energy and gamma rays at the upper end are high energy. These various types of energy are different in wavelengths but all are forms of electromagnetic radiation.

The electromagnetic spectrum is the full range of light in all of its forms, visible and invisible. When viewed along a spectrum, such as the one pictured below, radio waves are very long. Television waves and radar waves are shorter. Radio waves may have wavelengths of half a mile or more. Microwave lengths may be a few centimeters long. Visible light wavelengths are a few ten thousandths of a single millimeter long. X-rays are a few millionths of a single millimeter. Gamma rays at the far end of the spectrum are even shorter.

WAVES AND PARTICLES

All forms of electromagnetic energy travel as waves of electric and magnetic fields. Electromagnetic radiation is made up of an electric field and a magnetic field at right angles to each other. Light and all other forms of electromagnetic radiation also travel as a stream of particles called **photons**. These photons are like tiny bursts of energy given off when charged particles lose energy.

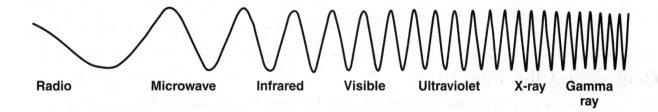

| Radio | Microwave | Infrared | Visible | Ultraviolet | X-ray | Gamma ray |

Unit
14

Electromagnetic Radiation

SOURCES OF ELECTROMAGNETIC ENERGY

Most electromagnetic energy comes to us from the universe beyond Earth. These waves can travel trough the emptiness of space unlike water or sound which need material to travel through. Huge amounts travel here from the Sun, but we also receive radiation from other stars and galaxies. The atmosphere above Earth absorbs large amounts of radiation, especially those that might be harmful. However, radio waves and light pass through the atmosphere.

COMMON CHARACTERISTICS

All forms of electromagnetic energy have several things in common. All types of electromagnetic radiation involve the transfer of energy from one place to another. Electromagnetic radiation in all of its forms does not need to have a medium—such as air, water, or metal—to travel through. All forms of radiation can and does travel through the **vacuum** of space.

All forms of electromagnetic radiation travel at exactly the same speed—the speed of light, 186,383 miles per second in the vacuum of space. All forms of electromagnetic radiation can be produced and absorbed by matter. For example, light can be produced by an electric light bulb and absorbed by some types of cloth. Electromagnetic energy does not carry an electric charge in any form. All forms of electromagnetic energy can be **reflected** and **refracted** just as light can be.

USES OF ELECTROMAGNETIC RADIATION

Radio waves and television waves are essential to modern communication. Radar is used to help planes and ships communicate and avoid dangers. Microwaves are used to cook food. Fluorescent lights use ultraviolet rays. Gamma rays are used in the treatment of disease. Visible light is essential to life on the planet.

VISIBLE LIGHT

Visible light is probably the most recognized form of electromagnetic energy. White light, such as sunlight, is composed of a range of seven colors called the *spectrum*. When light is passed through a **prism**, these seven colors become visible. They are red, orange, yellow, green, blue, indigo, and violet. Each color has a different wavelength with red being the longest and violet the shortest. Water is a natural prism that bends sunlight producing a rainbow with the seven colors of the spectrum.

Electromagnetic Radiation

LIGHT: REFLECTION AND REFRACTION

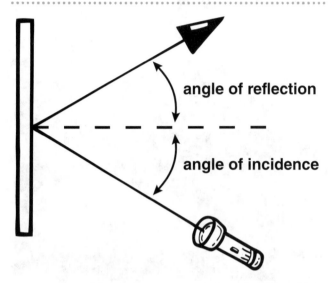

angle of reflection

angle of incidence

angle of incidence = angle of reflection

Light can be tightly focused by using convex lenses and spread out by using concave lenses. Visible light can be reflected by using mirrors or other smooth, shiny, reflective materials. The angle at which light strikes a mirror is exactly equal to the angle at which it reflects off the mirror. This is expressed in mathematical terms as the angle of incidence equals the angle of reflection. If light strikes a mirror at a 60° angle, it will be reflected off the mirror at a 60° angle.

Light can be blocked by dark, solid objects. A shadow is created when light does not go through a solid object. Light passes through objects that are transparent. Light can be refracted by passing through different types of transparent materials. Light changes speed and direction when it passes from one material to another kind of transparent material. When light passes from air to a denser material, such as water or glass, it slows down and is bent. The more it is slowed down, the greater the angle at which it is bent.

Facts to Remember

● *The electromagnetic spectrum includes radio waves, television waves, radar waves, microwaves, infrared rays, visible light, ultraviolet rays, x-rays, and gamma rays.*

● *This electromagnetic radiation travels both as waves and as a stream of particles.*

● *Most electromagnetic radiation comes from the Sun and stars.*

● *Electromagnetic radiation does not need to travel through a medium. It can travel through the vacuum of space.*

● *All forms of electromagnetic radiation travel at the speed of light.*

● *Electromagnetic radiation does not carry a charge.*

● *Visible light consists of seven colors of the spectrum: red, orange, yellow, green, blue, indigo, and violet.*

● *Light can be focused, reflected, and refracted.*

VOCABULARY

electromagnetic radiation—*forms of wave energy; forms of light*

photons—*particles of energy*

prism—*a triangular piece of glass used to show the spectrum*

reflect—*to bounce light off*

refract—*to bend light*

spectrum—*a range of colors or wavelengths*

vacuum—*empty of matter, including air*

Examining X-rays

Materials
- *x-rays obtained from medical labs, hospitals, veterinarians, and families in the community*
- *books and other sources showing the bone structure of humans (or animals if the x-rays come from animal labs)*

Directions

This activity works well with teams of two or three students.

1. Carefully examine the x-ray you have been given.
2. Draw a sketch showing all of the bones and other features visible on the x-ray.

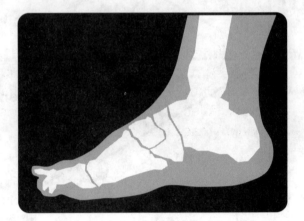

3. Find books, Internet sites, or other resources displaying the names of the bones visible on the x-ray.
4. Label as many bones or features on your sketch as you can find in books or other sources.

Try This

Carefully study the x-ray looking for damage that might be visible to bones or other features. The x-ray might show broken bones, diseased bones, growths, or other features that would not be normal to a healthy person or animal. Look for rings, pacemakers, or metal pieces on the x-ray. What did you find?

_____

_____

Hands and Feet

1. Find an x-ray of a hand or foot to share with your partners and count the number of bones.

_____

2. Draw a sketch and label all the bones whose names you can find.

Understanding Electromagnetic Radiation

Directions

This activity can be done in teams of two to four students.

1. Cut out each of the nine cards.
2. Study each of the cards.
3. Take turns with a partner testing your recognition of each form of electromagnetic radiation.
4. Switch partners and test each other again.

CARD #1
Radio Waves
Sources:
  stars (Sun)
  black holes
  radio broadcasts
 	
Uses:
  Communication
	CARD #2
	Television Waves
	Sources:
	  stars (Sun)
	  television broadcasts
	
	Uses:
	  Communication
		CARD #3
		Radar Waves
		Sources:
		  stars (Sun)
		  transmitters
		
		Uses:
		  Locating objects

CARD #4
Microwaves
Sources:
  stars (Sun)
  electron beams
    (from magnetron)
Uses:
  Communication
  Cooking
	CARD #5
	Infrared Rays
	Sources:
	  stars (Sun)
	  chemical action
	  living creatures
	Uses:
	  Heating
	  Cooking
	  Plant growth
		CARD #6
		Visible Light
		Sources:
		  stars (Sun)
		  chemical action
		  some creatures
		Uses:
		  Navigation
		  Vision
		  Plant growth

CARD #7
Ultraviolet Rays
Sources:
  stars (Sun)
 	
Uses:
  Chemical reactions
  Skin health
  Damage skin
	CARD #8
	X-rays
	Sources:
	  stars
	  bombarding atoms
	
	Uses:
	  Killing tumors
	  Chest x-ray
		CARD #9
		Gamma Rays
		Sources:
		  star explosions
		  black holes
		  nuclear reactions
		Uses:
		  Damage skin
		  Skin treatments

Using Prisms

Materials
- *plastic triangular prism*
- *flashlight*
- *cardboard boxes (optional)*
- *white paper*
- *black paper*
- *pushpin*
- *rubber band or masking tape*
- *colored pencils or markers*

Directions

The room must be dark for this activity to work well. This activity can be done in teams of two to four students.

1. Use a piece of black construction paper to cover the bulb of the flashlight. Use masking tape or a rubber band to hold it in place.
2. Use a pushpin or the tip of a pencil to make a small hole in the center of the black paper covering the bulb.
3. Make the room as dark as possible or do the experiment inside a cardboard box where you can block out the light.
4. One partner should shine the beam of light at the prism.
5. The second partner should hold the white paper on the other side of the prism.
6. Adjust the prism, flashlight, and white paper until you see the colors of the spectrum.

Recording Results

Which colors of the spectrum did you see? _____

_____

What did you have to do to make the most colors visible? _____

_____

Draw a sketch of the project and use colored pencils or markers to illustrate the spectrum you produced.

Try This

Make a larger hole in the cover over the flashlight. Shine it through the prism.

Describe the results. _____

_____

Draw a sketch with the spectrum showing on the white paper.

Using Prisms

Use this page with page 118. This activity can be done in teams of two to four students. The room must be dark for this activity to work well.

Materials
- *plastic triangular prisms*
- *flashlight*
- *cardboard boxes (optional)*
- *white paper*
- *black paper*
- *pushpin*
- *rubber band or masking tape*
- *colored pencils or markers*

Using Two Prisms

1. Arrange two prisms in as many different ways as you can. Shine the flashlight beam through the prisms together.
2. Draw a sketch of each arrangement, color the spectrum produced, and describe the results.

Arrangement #1
Description:

Sketch

_____

_____

_____

_____

Arrangement #2
Description:

Sketch

_____

_____

_____

Arrangement #3
Description:

Sketch

_____

_____

_____

_____

Arrangement #4
Description:

Sketch

_____

_____

_____

_____

Can You Do This?

Can you arrange the two prisms so that the beam of light goes into one prism, makes a spectrum, continues through the other prism, and exits as white light?

Water Prisms

Materials
- *clear plastic cup or drinking glass*
- *white paper*
- *scissors*
- *water*
- *flashlight*
- *colored pencils or markers*
- *shoebox*
- *black paper*

Directions: Sunlight Prism

This activity can be done in teams of two to four students.

1. Cut a piece of black construction paper about four inches by six inches.
2. Use the scissors to cut a 1-centimeter wide by three inches long piece in the center of the black paper.
3. Fill a drinking glass or a clear, plastic cup with water.
4. Tape the black paper to the glass or cup.
5. Place the cup next to a window with exposure to the sun. The black paper slit should be next to the window.
6. Lay a piece of white paper in front of the cup.

Recording Results

Describe what you saw. _____

Draw a sketch of the spectrum with colored pencils or markers.

Water Prism in a Box

1. Make a cut at one end of a shoebox like you did with the black paper.
2. Cover the bottom of the box with white paper.
3. Place the glass or clear plastic cup of water next to the slit.
4. Cut a flap on the top or side of the shoebox so that you can lift up to see in without letting in light from the room.
5. Hold the flashlight against the cut at the end of the shoebox.
6. Lift the flap and observe what happened.

Try This

Cut an opening in the other end of the box and place another cup of water at that end. Shine a flashlight at both ends. Observe what happens.

Making a Periscope

Materials
- *two small mirrors*
- *masking tape*
- *long, thin rectangular box (aluminum foil box or shoebox)*
- *flashlight*
- *black paper*
- *pushpin*
- *cardboard box (optional)*

Directions: Experimenting with Mirrors

This activity can be done in teams of two to four students.

1. Use a piece of black construction paper to cover the bulb of the flashlight. Use masking tape to hold it in place.
2. Use a pushpin (or the tip of a pencil) to make a small hole in the center of the black paper covering the bulb.
3. Make the room as dark as possible or do the experiment inside a cardboard box where you can block out room light.
4. One partner should shine the beam of light at one mirror at an angle.
5. The second partner should position another mirror to catch the reflection.
6. Do several different mirror arrangements. Sketch the results of each arrangement.

First Arrangement	Second Arrangement
Third Arrangement	Fourth Arrangement

Making a Periscope

1. Cover the inside of a long, thin cardboard box—such as an aluminum foil box—with black paper. A shoebox will also work.
2. Tape a small mirror at the top of the box at a 45° angle.
3. Tape a small mirror at the bottom of the box at a 45° angle facing the mirror at the top.
4. Cut a hole about one inch deep and one to two inches wide in from of the top mirror.
5. Cut a hole about one inch deep and one to two inches wide at the bottom on the opposite side facing the bottom mirror as shown in the illustration.

Using the Periscope

Use the periscope to see around corners, over desks, and into awkward places.

Student Inquiry Activity

Possible Inquiries

- What can you learn about the human body from examining x-rays?
- What parts of the human body can you identify using x-rays?
- How does a telescope use light to help you see?
- What is the darkest shadow you can make?
- Can you make rainbows with colored water and sunlight?
- Can you make rainbows with a flashlight, mirrors, and water?
- Can you make a rainbow with snow?
- Can you make a double or triple rainbow?
- Can you make a model of the refraction of light from air to water to glass?
- What differences can you discover when you refract light in water, alcohol, clear glass, clear plastic, colored water, and oil?
- Can you make a model of the waves of each type of electromagnetic radiation?
- Can you reflect one beam of light off a series of two, three, and four mirrors?
- Can you make a model of how long it would take you to travel to various objects in space at the speed of light?

Your Ideas

List your ideas for an inquiry investigation about electromagnetic radiation.

1. _____
2. _____
3. _____

Possible Inquiry on Electromagnetic Radiation

1. Read the inquiry suggestions listed above.
2. Choose one of those suggestions or an inquiry idea of your own and write down your choice.
3. List the problems you will encounter and tell how you will solve them.

Your Inquiry: _____

_____

Possible Problems: _____

_____

Possible Solutions: _____

_____

Use the Student Inquiry Worksheets for guidance and to record data.

Focus on a Scientist: Albert Einstein

Albert Einstein was the greatest scientist and the most important physicist since Isaac Newton. He fundamentally changed modern scientists' understanding of the universe, and his work sparked debates that have furthered human knowledge in math, astronomy, chemistry, and physics.

Einstein was born in 1879 in Ulm, Germany and was brought up in Munich, Germany. He did not talk until he was three years old, and his eccentric personal traits became obvious in his childhood. School was easy for him, but he did not like the structure and discipline. Einstein understood math with extraordinary clarity, but he would make careless mistakes that earned him poor grades. He often preferred to be alone and had few friends. He played the violin in public parks sometimes and enjoyed studying physics and math. Albert was less interested in other sciences and languages. He eventually entered an institute to prepare him to teach.

Einstein spent his spare time studying physics while working as a clerk in a patent office in Switzerland where inventions were recorded and the rights of the inventor were protected. He also fell in love with a brilliant physics student named Mileva Maric. They had three children.

In 1905, Albert Einstein published four revolutionary papers in Germany's most important physics journal. One paper gave a detailed and convincing proof for the existence of atoms and molecules. These concepts are essential to modern chemistry and physics. Another paper dealt with the nature of light waves. Einstein made the revolutionary assertion that light traveled both as waves and particles. This paper was very controversial until his theories were confirmed in 1919 by a study of the movement of light during a solar eclipse.

The most widely disputed paper was his Special Theory of Relativity in which he argued that time, distance, and mass can all change depending on how fast you are moving. Later, Einstein would expand this theory into a General Theory of Relativity—he proved that energy and mass are different forms of the same thing. His famous equation expresses this discovery: $E = mc^2$. This equation states that energy is equal to mass times the speed of light times the speed of light again. This equation was useful, especially in the study of atoms and molecules and the understanding of time and space.

In his later life, Einstein left Switzerland and later Germany to settle in the United States at Princeton University. Even though he was generally opposed to war, he suggested to President Roosevelt the need to develop an atomic bomb, because Hitler's German scientists were working on a similar weapon. He divorced his first wife and married a cousin in 1919. He spent the remainder of his life in Princeton where he died in 1955.

Sound

DID YOU KNOW THAT . . . ?

- *Sound waves pile up in front of a jet aircraft when it travels faster than the speed of sound. These waves cause a shock wave and a sonic boom that can be heard on the ground.*

- *A singer who sings at the exact same frequency of a wine glass can burst the glass.*

- *Bats produce and hear ultrahigh frequency sounds.*

- *Dolphins use ultrasound frequencies when communicating with each other and to navigate through the ocean like ships using sonar.*

SOUND ENERGY

Sound is not a form of electromagnetic energy, but it does travel in waves. Sound is a form of energy produced by vibrating objects. These **vibrations** have two motions. First, vibrations push the air forward pressing the molecules of air together. The second motion pulls the air back causing the air to expand. These cycles of compression and expansion are vibrations that travel through the air as sound waves. The speed of sound in air is about 770 miles per hour depending upon the temperature of the air and the altitude above sea level. Sound waves cannot travel at all through a vacuum-like space.

SPEED OF SOUND

Sound waves can travel through many materials, such as air, water, wood, glass, metals, and most other materials. Sound waves travel faster through dense materials with closely packed molecules. Sound travels through warm air at 1,130 feet per second. Sound travels about 40 feet per second slower in cold, freezing air. Sound travels almost 5,000 feet per second through warm water and more than 600 feet per second slower in water at the freezing point. It travels more than 20,000 feet per second through steel.

Some materials are useful in insulating buildings to keep sound out because sound waves travel very slowly through them. It travels only 177 feet per second through rubber. Soft, cushion-like material, such as cloth and some kinds of foam, mute sounds. Heavy curtains on a stage, tapestries on walls, and large numbers of people tend to absorb sounds.

Speed of Sound

Material	Feet Per Second	Miles Per Hour
warm air	1,130	770
cold air	1,086	740
warm water	5,000	3,409
cold water	4,213	2,873
steel	20,000	13,636
oak wood	3,850	2,625
rubber	177	121
glass	16,404	11,185

Sound

FREQUENCY

Sound waves traveling through air have different frequencies and different wavelengths. The **frequency** or **pitch** of a sound is determined by the number of vibrations in a single second. A sound that produces many cycles of compression and expansion in one second has a higher frequency than one that produces fewer vibrations. High frequency sounds have shorter wavelengths and more wavelengths than those of lower frequency. Frequencies are measured in standard units called **hertz** which is abbreviated Hz. One hertz is equal to one vibration in one second. A kilohertz is equal to 1,000 vibrations per second. A megahertz is equal to one million vibrations per second. The hertz was named in honor of Heinrich Hertz who discovered radio waves.

FREQUENCY RANGES

Sound waves can have frequencies as low as one hertz and as high as 150,000Hz. The human voice can produce sounds in frequencies as low 85Hz and as high as 1,100Hz. However, they can hear a much wider range of frequencies, between about 20Hz and 20,000Hz. Higher frequencies cannot be heard. Many animals can hear at higher frequencies than humans. A dog whistle has a frequency so high that dogs can hear it but not humans. A dog can hear between 15Hz and 50,000Hz, even though it can only make sounds between about 500Hz and 1,000Hz. Grasshoppers can make chirping sounds as high as 100,000Hz. Bats hear from 1,000Hz to 120,000Hz. Porpoises can hear up to 150,000Hz. Ultrasound scanners used in medicine to study unborn children can achieve over 7,000,000Hz.

PITCH AND MUSIC

Pitch is the term used in music to describe frequency. The higher the number of sound waves per second, the higher the frequency and pitch. Musical notes on an instrument have very exact measurements. For example, middle C has a precise frequency of 256Hz. Musical instruments produce different ranges of frequency. For example, a piano ranges from a low of 30Hz to a high of 4,100Hz. A violin only has a range of 200Hz to 2,650Hz. A pipe organ can have a range as high as 8,000Hz.

Hertz Chart

	Frequency Produced	Frequency Heard
Child	85Hz to 1,100Hz	20Hz to 20,000Hz
60-year-old man	85Hz to 1,100Hz	20Hz to 12,000Hz
Bat	10,000Hz to 120,000Hz	1,000Hz to 120,000Hz
Dog	450Hz to 1,080Hz	15Hz to 50,000Hz

Sound

LOUDNESS

The loudness of sound depends upon the intensity or energy carried by the waves of sound. Huge vibrations have a lot of energy and intensity. They produce large sound waves and great differences between the high and low points of a sound wave. All sounds travel at the same speed, but the size of the waves will vary a great deal.

THE DECIBEL SCALE

The loudness of sound is measured in **decibels**, a term created in honor of Alexander Graham Bell, inventor of the telephone and longtime student of the science of sound. The scale shown below presents some typical sounds and their rating on the decibel scale. The scale is a logarithmic scale meaning that every 10 points on the scale is 10 times louder than the preceding 10. For example, a decibel level of 40 is 10 times a level of 30 and 100 times a level of 20. So the sound of a restaurant at 70 dB is 1,000,000 times as loud as the sound of a falling leaf at 10 dB.

Regular exposure to sounds above 80 decibels will damage human ears. Constant exposure to decibel levels at 90 dB or above can cause permanent hearing damage. Exposure to sounds over 120 dB will cause pain. Human eardrums can burst at 140 decibels. A broken eardrum will result in deafness until it has grown back. There is some variation in decibel levels based on the intensity of the sound.

Decibel Scale	
140 dB	Rocket launch; gunshots
130 dB	Fire sirens; motorcycles right next to you
120 dB	Jet aircraft taking off
110 dB	Chainsaw; thunder
100 dB	Rock concert; firecrackers; garbage truck; subway
90 dB	Very busy street traffic; car horns; lawn mowers
80 dB	Pneumatic drill digging up street; orchestra
70 dB	Vacuum cleaner; street traffic; noisy restaurant
60 dB	Normal conversation
50 dB	average home or office with people working
40 dB	Quiet office; library; humming refrigerator
30 dB	People whispering
20 dB	Soft breathing
10 dB	A falling leaf
0 dB	Threshold for human hearing

Sound

HOW YOUR EAR HEARS

Human ears collect sound waves. Human ears, like those of most mammals, have three distinct regions or parts. When sound waves enter a human ear, they travel through the outer ear as if through a funnel until they strike the eardrum. The waves of sound make the eardrum vibrate back and forth. The vibrations are then carried by three bones in the middle ear called **ossicles**. They make the sounds louder.

The vibrations are transmitted to the inner ear where the fluid in the inner ear, called the *cochlea*, starts to vibrate. These vibrations are picked up by very sensitive cells and are sent as electric signals along nerves to the brain that translates them into messages. The force of the sound as it travels through the ear can be twenty times greater than the original vibrations picked up by the eardrum.

Facts to Know

- Sound travels in waves.

- Sound waves are created by vibrating objects.

- The speed of sound varies depending upon the medium it is traveling through.

- The frequency of a sound is measured by the number of vibrations per second.

- Frequency of vibrations is measured in hertz (Hz).

- Animals vary greatly in their ability to hear high frequencies.

- Loudness is measured on the decibel scale.

- Sounds above 90 dB can cause permanent damage.

- Human ears collect and magnify sounds.

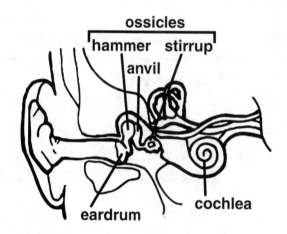

VOCABULARY

decibel—*a measurement for the loudness of sound*

frequency—*the number of vibrations per second; sometimes called pitch*

hertz—*the measurement of frequency in vibrations per second megahertz (one million hertz)*

ossicles—*three tiny bones in the middle ear*

pitch—*musical term for frequency*

vibrations—*sound waves created by the movement of objects*

Working with Decibels

Directions: Study the decibel chart on page 126. Place the noises listed here in the appropriate place on the decibel chart. (Some answers will vary because decibel levels are approximations, and they are affected by how close a person is to the noise.)

Decibel Levels

140 dB _____

130 dB _____

120 dB _____

110 dB _____

100 dB _____

90 dB _____

80 dB _____

70 dB _____

60 dB _____

50 dB _____

40 dB _____

30 dB _____

20 dB _____

10 dB _____

0 dB _____

playground whistle	jet plane overhead	soft breathing
honking car horns	motorcycles	normal conversation
quiet office	humming refrigerator	barking dog
crying baby	heavy metal concert	phone ringing
threshold for human hearing	lawn mower	gunshots
chainsaw	jackhammer	ice cream truck
playground whistle	vacuum cleaner	snow plow
garbage truck	exciting football game	car alarm
train locomotive	fire truck with alarm	helicopter (close)
whispering	leaf blower	jet aircraft taking off
noisy restaurant	library	teen dance
television show	CD player—full volume	firecrackers
falling leaf	loud snoring	police siren
rocket launch	thunder (close)	full orchestra
fire sirens	cat meowing	moderate street traffic
tractor	subway	cheerleaders leading school
average home or office	very busy street traffic	

Fishline Phone

> **Materials**
> • *fishline* • *8 oz. or 10 oz. plastic cups* • *scissors* • *pushpin* • *small paper clips*

Making the Phone

1. Cut a piece of nylon fishline about 15 feet long.
2. Use a pushpin to make a hole in the bottom of each of two 8 oz. or 10 oz. plastic cups.
3. Thread one end of the fishline through the bottom of one cup and tie one small paper clip to the line.
4. Pull the line and paper clip firmly against the inside bottom of the cup.
5. Thread the other end of the fishline through the bottom of the second cup, tie another small paper clip to the line, and pull it firmly against the inside bottom of the cup.

Using the Phone

• One partner should hold the cup over one ear while the other talks into the cup. The line must be kept tight, or the phone will not work. What can you hear? _____

_____

• One partner can also tap on his cup to see if the listening partner can hear the tapping.

How It Works

The speaker's voice vibrates molecules of air inside the cup. These vibrations are picked up by the bottom of the cup acting as a diaphragm. The line transfers the vibrations to the bottom of the second cup acting as a diaphragm that vibrates the molecules of air in the second cup. These vibrations are then heard by the ear of the listener.

Try This

What happens if you pinch the line while someone is talking? _____

_____

What happens if the line touches a chair, a wall, or another person? _____

_____

Will the phone work if the line gets a tangled knot in it? _____

_____

Will the phone work if the line is allowed to get loose? _____

_____

Why do you think the line must be tight? _____

_____

Party Line—Four Way Conversations

Materials
fishline phone used on page 129 or 133

Directions

Use this page with page 133. This activity requires teams of four or six students. This activity works best outside.

1. Find an open space on the playground.

2. One set of partners should move apart until their phone lines are stretched tight when they try to talk and hear.

3. The second set of partners should stand at right angles to the first partners.

4. The lines should cross.

5. One partner from the second pair must wrap his or her cup and fishline around the first line to keep the lines in contact.

6. Each of the four students holds one cup so that the line remains tight and not touching anything else.

7. Three students listen while one student talks.

8. Try different ways of speaking into the cup so that all listeners can hear clearly.

9. Describe how well the party line worked. _____

_____

Making Improvements

• Use a piece of fishline 20 or 25 feet long to make a longer phone.

• Connect your phone set with a pair of partners.

• Test your phone set. Describe how well this party line worked. _____

_____

Six Way Conversations

Find a third set of partners. Arrange your three phone sets so that all the lines are connected by wrapping the third set around the lines of the first two sets.

Describe how well this six-way party line worked.

_____

_____

_____

Making Music

Materials
- *5 to 8 glass bottles*
- *food coloring*
- *water and pitcher*
- *pencil or metal spoon*
- *ruler*

Directions

1. Arrange your bottles in a straight line where they will be safe and not fall.

2. Fill a pitcher with water and add a few drops of food coloring so that the water will be more visible in the glass bottles.

3. Pour water into the first bottle until it is two centimeters high. Use a ruler to check exact heights.

4. Fill the second bottle four centimeters high with the colored water.

5. Fill the third bottle six centimeters high.

6. Fill the fourth bottle eight centimeters high.

7. Fill the fifth bottle 10 centimeters high.

8. If you have them, fill the sixth bottle with 12 centimeters, the seventh with 14 centimeters, and the last with 16 centimeters of water.

Using the Instrument

This arrangement of bottles can provide a variety of sounds like a xylophone.

- Use a pencil to strike each bottle at the top in order from low to high water.

- Listen for the different tone in each sound.

- Try using a metal spoon.

Which sounds clearer and better—the pencil or the spoon? _____

Blow gently across the top of each bottle the way the ancient Greeks blew across the top of panpipes. What was the sound like? _____

_____

Can you plan a simple song or make up a song using the bottles? Make charts showing the tunes you made with the lowest shown as number 1.

It might look like this.

Sample: 1 3 5 2 2 1 1 5 4 4 1

First tune: ___ ___ ___ ___ ___ ___ ___ ___ ___ ___ ___

Second tune: ___ ___ ___ ___ ___ ___ ___ ___ ___ ___ ___

Bouncing Sound

Materials
- *2 long cardboard tubes or 4 short paper towel roll tubes*
- *stiff card, metal tray, thin wooden board, or similar item*
- *masking tape*
- *ticking clock or party sound maker*

Directions

This experiment works best with a team of two or three students.

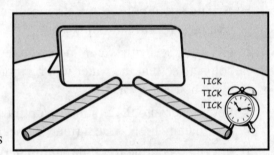

1. Stand or tape a metal tray, stiff card, plastic tray, thin wooden board, aluminum cooking pan, or similar material upright on a desk or table.

2. Find two long wrapping paper tubes or poster tubes. Tape together two paper towel roll tubes if no long tubes are available.

3. Place the two long tubes with one opening against the card or tray as shown in the illustration.

4. Place a ticking clock at the end of one tube away from the card. If you don't have a clock, a student can tap or scratch on the end of one tube with a fingernail, coin, or pencil.

5. Listen for the sound at the open end of the other tube. What did it sound like?

_____

_____

6. Have partners take turns listening and whispering into the tubes. Describe what you heard.

_____

_____

Try This

- Use different boards, cards, pans, or trays to see which material reflected the sounds best from one tube to another. Describe your observations.

_____

- Try using party sound makers, finger snaps, and mouth sounds. Which worked best?

_____

- How far away from each other can you move the tubes and still hear the sounds?

_____

- Try other materials as the reflecting board or tray, such as books, construction paper, and styrofoam. Did any soft materials work well?

_____

_____

- What did you learn from this activity?

_____

_____

Student Inquiry Activity

Use page 130 as a lead-in to this activity. This activity works best with a team of two students.

Inquiry Project: How Can You Make A Better Phone?

Use the suggested materials or any others you wish to improve the design and effectiveness of your fishline phone.

Thinking About Volume and Sound Quality

1. Make new phone sets using several of these suggestions.
   - cardboard coffee cups
   - paper cups
   - large plastic cups
   - styrofoam cups
   - giant-sized 32 oz. cups
   - empty soup cans
   - empty family-size tin cans
   - empty aluminum cans
   - other large cups or containers
   - giant vegetable cans from the school cafeteria

2. Try out your new set. Can you hear as well or better with the new set? _____
   _____

3. Try different ways of speaking into this set. Is it better to shout, talk inside the cup, speak
   normally, whisper, or speak outside the mouth of the cup? Why? _____
   _____

4. Which set worked best? Why? _____
   _____

Going for Distance

1. To increase the distance your phone will work, try using these materials:
   - longer fishline   • different kinds of string   • different kinds of thin wire
2. Try different ways of speaking into the cup.
3. Try speaking entirely inside the cup.
4. Try shouting into the cup.
5. Try speaking in a normal voice near the opening of the cup.
6. Tap the cup with your fingers.
7. Scratch the cup with a fingernail or coin.

Which sounds could be heard best by the listener? _____
_____

Which sounds were muffled? _____

Completing the Inquiry

Use the Student Inquiry Worksheets to complete all the parts of this inquiry.

Great Scientific Discoveries

DID YOU KNOW THAT . . . ?

- *Alexander Graham Bell was trying to improve the telegraph when he invented the telephone.*

- *Benjamin Franklin invented the rocking chair, bifocal glasses, a better stove, and proved that lightning is a form of electricity.*

- *Michael Faraday was originally hired by the famous chemist Sir Humphry Davy to wash bottles. In his lifetime, Faraday made more discoveries than Davy.*

HUBBLE'S LAW: THE EXPANDING UNIVERSE

American astronomer Edwin Hubble studied the Andromeda Nebula, a **galaxy** not far from the Milky Way galaxy of which we are a part. In the 1920s, he found that the light emitted from this galaxy and other nearby galaxies was at the red end of the spectrum. This indicated that these galaxies were moving away from us at tremendous speed. This information is the basis for Hubble's belief that the universe is expanding and became known as Hubble's Law. He also discovered that the farther away a galaxy is, the faster it is moving.

GEORGES LEMAITRE: THE BIG BANG THEORY

In 1927, Georges Lemaitre, a Belgian scientist, suggested that the universe began as a dense ball of matter that exploded in a "big bang," creating the universe. This idea seemed to fit in with Hubble's discoveries. In the 1960s, physicists discovered background microwave radiation that supported this theory that is generally accepted by most astronomers today.

GALILEO GALILEI: LAWS OF FALLING BODIES

Galileo conducted many careful experiments on inclined planes to determine how objects fell. He may also have performed an experiment from the Tower of Pisa where he dropped two objects of the same size but of different weights. All of his experiments proved that objects fall at the same speed, regardless of weight. Objects gain speed as they fall. This is true in a vacuum. Air resistance may affect the speed of falling bodies if the shape of the object is slowed by air.

Great Scientific Discoveries

LOUIS PASTEUR: THE GERM THEORY OF DISEASE

Louis Pasteur was a chemist who became interested in the causes of diseases in humans and animals. He discovered that **microorganisms** not only caused disease but that they could be killed. He invented treatments for cholera, anthrax, and rabies. He invented a process for sterilizing beer and wine. This process called **pasteurization** is widely used for milk and other foods today.

ALESSANDRO VOLTA: THE BATTERY

Alessandro Volta was an Italian scientist who studied electricity and invented the first chemical battery. In 1800, he alternated disks of copper and zinc in a salt solution and produced an electric current. It thus became possible to produce, store, and use electricity in a practical way.

MICHAEL FARADAY: MAGNETISM CAN BE CONVERTED TO ELECTRICITY

Michael Faraday was a very practical scientist who deliberately set out to prove that a magnet could produce electric current when the magnet was turned within a coil of wire. He also proved that electric current had a magnetic effect. This idea of electromagnetic induction is the basis of the electric generator and the electric motor.

JAMES CLERK MAXWELL: PREDICTED THE ELECTROMAGNETIC SPECTRUM

Maxwell wrote Faraday's discoveries in a mathematical formulation that explained precisely how electric and magnetic fields behave. These equations suggested the existence of electromagnetic waves and the electromagnetic spectrum as well as the movement of these electric and magnetic fields vibrating at right angles to each other and moving at the speed of light.

DANIEL BERNOULLI: BERNOULLI'S PRINCIPLE

Daniel Bernoulli was a Swiss doctor and mathematician who did a lot of experiments with fluids and gases. The principle he discovered was that when the speed of a liquid or gas increased, the pressure dropped. When air flows over the curved upper surface of an airplane wing, it moves faster because it is covering more distance than when it moves over the flat undersurface of the wing. Air pressure is therefore less on top of the wing and proportionally greater under the wing. This creates an upward lift for the plane.

Great Scientific Discoveries

LOUIS AGASSIZ: GLACIERS ARE CAUSED BY ICE AGES

Louis Agassiz was a **naturalist** on vacation in the Alps when his observations caused him to suggest that the damage done to the rocks was caused by **glaciers**. He suggested that there had been many ice ages and that glaciers were the results of these periodic ice ages. Today scientists believe that there have been as many as 17 ice ages in the last 600 million years. The last ice age began about two million years ago and at times covered up to 30% of the surface of Earth. Presently, Earth is in an interglacial period and ice covers about 10% of its surface.

CARL LINNAEUS: SYSTEM OF CLASSIFICATION

Linnaeus was a Swedish botanist who studied plants and animals, even as a young boy. He described and named nearly 8,000 plants and 4,400 animal species which were known in the 1700s when he was alive. He invented the basis of the system of classification now used. His two-name system included the genus and the species written in Latin, then the universal language of science.

BLAISE PASCAL: PASCAL'S LAW

Pascal was a brilliant mathematician and scientist of the 1600s who invented a kind of calculator at the age of 20. He studied the impact of fluids under pressure and discovered that pressure is transmitted equally in all directions when applied to a fluid. This is called *Pascal's Law*. Hydraulic pressure is used today in many applications. This principle helps raise cars in an auto repair shop and explains why balloons swell evenly when air is forced into them.

Facts to Remember

- *The universe was created in an explosion called the "Big Bang."*
- *Objects of different weights fall at the same speed in a vacuum.*
- *Electricity can produce magnetic effects and magnets can produce electricity.*
- *The electromagnetic spectrum travels in waves at the speed of light.*
- *Microorganisms can cause disease in humans and animals.*
- *There have been many ice ages on Earth.*
- *All living organisms have a two-name classification.*
- *Pressure on fluids is applied equally in all directions.*

VOCABULARY

galaxy—*an independent system of stars*
glacier—*a huge sheet of ice*
naturalist—*a scientist who studies nature*
microorganisms—*extremely small living things; germs*
pasteurization—*a process for protecting food from contamination*

Airfoils and Planes

Bernoulli's Principle explains the way an airfoil works and how lift is accomplished in an airplane.

Materials
- *strips of thin paper*
- *ruler*
- *scissors*
- *8½ by 11 inch paper*
- *small paper clips*

Making an Airfoil

1. Cut a strip of paper two inches wide and 10 inches long.
2. Wrap the paper around a pencil so that it sticks out as shown in the illustration.
3. Blow across the top half of the paper with a steady burst of air.
4. The paper should lift as you blow because the speed of the air is greater over the top of the airfoil than underneath.

Making a Paper Plane

You should get the same lift in this paper plane design because all of the folds make the top of the plane curved and the bottom flat.

1. Fold the top of an 8½ by 11 inch paper two inches down from the top.
2. Fold two inches more down from the first fold.
3. Make a third fold two inches more down from the top.
4. Fold the paper along the center so that the model is symmetrical.
5. Draw a line one inch from the centerfold on both sides of the fold.
6. Fold up along these centerlines to create a fuselage.

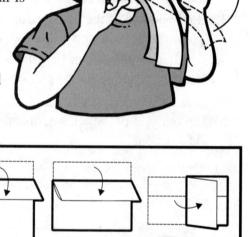

7. Measure half inch in from the edges of the model and draw a line along each edge.
8. Fold up along these edges to create the rudders or stabilizers of the plane.

Flying the Plane

- Launch your paper flyer by holding the fuselage between your thumb and middle finger. Your forefinger will be held against the rear of the plane. Use a flick of your wrist to get it into the air.
- Try using a small paper clip on the nose of the plane.

Using a Galvanometer

Materials
- *magnetic directional compass*
- *battery*
- *thin electrical wire*
- *rough sandpaper or scissors*
- *nail*
- *ruler*

Directions

A galvanometer proves the existence of a magnetic effect produced by electricity.

1. Wrap a one-foot long piece of thin, insulated wire around the center of a magnetic directional compass. Leave two inches of wire at each end.

2. Use rough sandpaper or scissors to strip or scrape one inch of plastic coating from each end of the wire.

3. Hold one end of the wire against one pole of the battery—either the top of the bottom (the positive or negative pole).

4. Touch the other end of the wire to the other pole of the battery. Describe what happened to the pointer on the magnetic directional compass.

_____

5. Tap one end of the wire against the pole of the battery. Describe what happened to the pointer in the compass.

_____

6. Tap the other end of the wire against the pole of the battery. Describe what happened to the pointer in the compass.

_____

7. Hold both ends of the wire against the poles of the battery. Describe what happened to the pointer in the compass.

_____

8. Reverse the poles of the battery that are touching the ends of the wires. Describe what happened to the pointer in the compass.

_____

Try This

- Wrap the foot-long piece of thin, insulated wire around a nail. Leave two inches of wire sticking out at each end.

- Place the nail point or head near the compass pointer.

- Hold one end of the wire against one pole of the battery and touch the other end of the wire to the other battery pole. Describe what happened.

_____

- Reverse the wires and describe what happened.

_____

- Reverse the ends of the nail near the pointer and describe what happened.

_____

Making a Model Battery

Materials

- *copper pennies*
- *paper towel*
- *warm water*
- *thin electrical wire*
- *scissors*
- *dimes*

- *aluminum foil*
- *salt*
- *clear plastic cup*
- *lemon juice*
- *rough sandpaper*
- *nickels*

- *flashlight bulb*
- *small open tube or tray*
- *vinegar*
- *earphone set*
- *tape*

Directions

These models are similar to the battery invented by Volta. Use this page with page 140.

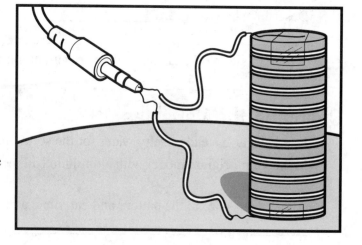

1. Cut out 10 aluminum foil circles about the size of a penny.
2. Cut out 10 circles from a paper towel about the size of a penny.
3. Cut two 6-inch long pieces of wire.
4. Use rough sandpaper or scissors to strip one inch of plastic coating from all four ends of the wire.
5. Stir one teaspoon of salt into a cup with three or four ounces of warm water.
6. Soak the circles in the warm, salty water.
7. Make a stack with a copper penny, a piece of wet paper towel, and an aluminum foil circle alternating in order. The stack will have a copper penny at one end and a foil circle at the other end. Use a small tray to help you hold the stack comfortably.

Making It Work

1. Connect the earphones over your ears.
2. Hold or tape one bare end of one wire to the first penny.
3. Hold or tape one bare end of the other wire to the last piece of foil.
4. Wrap one of the remaining wire ends around the plug or jack of the earphones.
5. Scrape the remaining bare end of the wire against the earphone jack.
6. Can you hear scratches, cracklings, or other strange noises made by the scraping wire?

Student Inquiry Activity

Directions

Use this page with page 139.

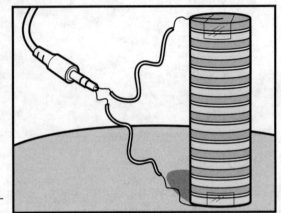

1. Study the model battery you made on page 139.
2. Make a new model battery using 10 pennies, 10 pieces of paper towel soaked in salty water, and 10 nickels.
3. Connect the earphones over your ears. Connect the wires to the ends of the stack as you did before.
4. Scrape the remaining bare end of the wire against the earphone jack.
5. Describe what you heard. _____
   _____
6. Which model worked better—the one with aluminum foil or the one with nickels?
   _____

Changing the Variables

1. Use vinegar instead of salty water for the solution.
2. Make your original model with aluminum foil, pennies, and paper towel soaked in vinegar instead of salty water.
3. Attach your wire to the battery and earphone as you did before. Describe how this model worked.
   _____
   _____
4. Add salt to the vinegar solution and soak the battery in the salty vinegar.
5. Attach this model to the earphone as you did before. Describe how this model worked. _____
   _____

Can You Light a Bulb?

Connect each of your model batteries to a flashlight bulb. Hold one wire end against the metal side of the bulb and the other wire end against the metal base of the bulb. How did each battery work?

Aluminum model: _____

Nickel model: _____

Vinegar model: _____

Vinegar and salt model: _____

Other Inquiries

- Try the same experiment using dimes, quarters, or thicker pieces of aluminum foil.
- Use lemon juice or grapefruit juice.
- Use the Student Inquiry Worksheets to complete this inquiry investigation.

Brainstorming and Selecting a Science Investigation

Selecting a good science investigation requires some careful thought and serious planning. Follow these steps to help you get started.

1. Make a list of the topics in science that interest you.

   _____

   _____

   _____

   _____

2. List the science materials you like to work with, such as batteries and wires, animals or plants, flying or floating objects, chemicals or liquids, or any other similar science supplies.

   _____

   _____

   _____

   _____

3. List ideas for science investigations in every area of interest. Use textbooks, science experiment books, Internet Web sites, other sources, and your own ideas.

   _____

   _____

   _____

   _____

4. Make a choice of one idea for your project. Use this checklist to help you.

   Is the project interesting and different?

   _____

   Is the project difficult enough but not too complicated for you to do?

   _____

   Can you find or purchase the necessary materials?

   _____

   What support will you need from your parents in getting the materials or making the model or experiment?

   _____

   Have you used some of your ideas to make the project interesting and unusual?

   _____

   Do you have the time to do the project?

   _____

5. Name and describe your chosen investigation.

   _____

   _____

Displaying and Presenting Your Science Investigation

Make your science investigation stand out by following these suggestions.

1. Write neatly or use a computer to print out your written investigation.

2. Use proper spelling, grammar, and appropriate science vocabulary on your write-up. Use your own sentences. Do not copy from a book.

3. Have plenty of data for your investigation. Do several trials, models, or experiments to prove your results.

4. Display your project on a folding cardboard display unit, on tagboard, or use stiff art paper.

5. Illustrate your project with drawings, outlines, or photos to help the viewer understand what you did.

6. Label and demonstrate your models or materials used in the investigation.

7. Prepare an oral presentation for your classmates, giving all of the details of your work and the results.

8. Carefully and clearly organize and list the results of each trial, experiment, model, or survey that you did.

9. State your conclusions clearly.

10. Evaluate your project. What could you have done to make the investigation better, more detailed, or clearer?

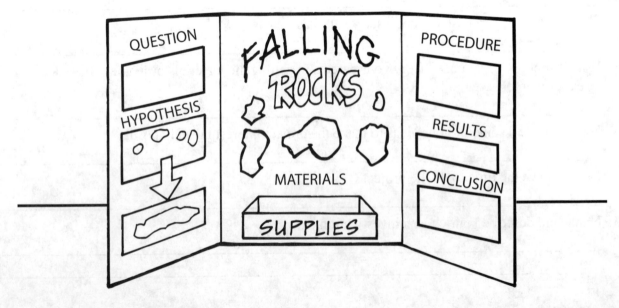

Science Investigation Format

Your investigation and display should follow the scientific method.

I. State a problem to be solved or investigated.

Examples: What happens to leaves covered from sunlight?

How does an electric circuit work?

What do mice really like to eat?

What colors make up white light?

II. Make a hypothesis (scientific guess) suggesting a possible solution to the problem or a plan of investigation.

Examples: Leaves need light to live.

Electric circuits must be connected.

Mice prefer peanut butter more than cheese.

There are several colors in white light.

III. Test your hypothesis using experimentation, models, and other investigations.

Examples: Cover several leaves on a plant for two weeks.

Create a variety of electric circuits.

Prepare a mouse diet and record mouse eating habits.

Use a prism and sunlight to refract light.

IV. Record your results.

Examples: Record the changes in the leaves every day.

Illustrate each electric circuit and describe whether it worked or didn't.

Keep a record of the mouse diet and what it ate.

Illustrate and describe the effect of sunlight passing through a prism.

V. State your conclusions.

Examples: Leaves can't survive without sunlight.

Electric circuits must be connected to a source of electricity and flow through conductors.

Mice prefer seeds more than peanut butter or cheese.

White light is composed of seven colors.

Science Investigation Worksheet

Use this worksheet and the information on page 143 to plan and do your science investigation.

I. State the problem to be solved or investigated. (What is the purpose of your investigation? What do you hope to prove, demonstrate, or find out?)

_____

_____

_____

II. Make a hypothesis (scientific guess) suggesting a possible solution to the problem or a plan of investigation. (What do you think is actually going to happen?)

_____

_____

_____

III. Test your hypothesis using experimentation, models, and other investigations. (What experiments will you try? What models are you going to make? What are you actually going to do to test your hypothesis?)

_____

_____

_____

_____

_____

IV. Record your results. (Keep an accurate, detailed, and complete record here of what happened in each investigation. Tell what happened and when it happened. Describe any changes and improvements you made. Draw pictures of the model or project you did.)

_____

_____

_____

_____

Illustration:

V. State your conclusions. (Tell what you learned.)

_____

_____